DINOSAUR THINKING

Domination

Territorialism

Blame

Lies

Impatience

Judgment

Fear

The SECRET of RIGHT RELATIONSHIPS

Overcoming Dinosaur Thinking

*Helping You Overcome
Your Compulsions and
Fears to Become
the Person God
Intends for You to Be*

DAVID DERBY

ANM
publishers

The SECRET of RIGHT RELATIONSHIPS
Overcoming Dinosaur Thinking

ISBN: 978-0-9715346-9-8 Paperback

Published by:

publishers

Advancing Native Missions
P.O. Box 5303 • Charlottesville, VA 22905
www.AdvancingNativeMissions.com

Written by:
David Derby
P.O. Box 202 • Saegertown, PA 16433 USA
DavidDerby@ZoomInternet.net • www.DavidDerby.net
Home Phone: 814-547-5812 • Cell: 814-573-2972

Edited by:
Colleen Derby, Betty Westmoreland, and Lora Zill

Scripture references are The Holy Bible, New International Version, 1978, by New York International Bible Society unless otherwise stated.

NOTE: The names and places in some of the stories have been changed or left out to protect identities.

ENDORSEMENTS

"I had the privilege of team teaching with Dr. David Derby to more than a 1,000 village grass root level Christian workers using the Indian edition of this book. (Dr. is an honorary title bestowed on David by tribal people throughout India.) I was saddened when the Indian immigration authorities denied him entrance into India in 2011. But praise the Lord that He has multiplied the Indian workers and missions that have caught his vision and use this book for discipleship, leadership, relationship, and Christian character education. Dr. Derby writes from his experiences and the leading of the Lord. As people learn what is in the book they see what is inside themselves. The simple messages tied into the Word of God will penetrate your heart. Hundreds of us in India are praying for the success of this book in America and other industrialized nations. We know it will bless you as it has blessed us, and proceeds from the sales of this book in America will go to underwrite much of the cost to continue our partnerships to reach all of the people groups in India."

Swapan Roy
Field Executive & Senior Audio Technician
Global Recordings Network, India
Disciples for the Harvest—India, Volunteer

"David Derby's work, *The Secret of Right Relationships: Overcoming Dinosaur Thinking*, uses the controlling metaphor of wrong-headed 'dinosaur thinking' to illustrate practical biblical truths about relationships. In this book, David Derby discusses in a very practical way the wrong behaviors of domination, territorialism, impatience, blame, complaining, lying, judging others, and fear. With abundant examples drawn from personal life experiences in his family, as a businessman, and as a speaker and missionary to India and elsewhere, David Derby is careful to ground each of his principles in the Scriptures. The work is replete with Scripture references for each point. This book has already been used in various settings as an excellent tool for discipleship and for strengthening relationships. It packs solid biblical truth into an easy-to-read format. I recommend it highly."

Todd S. Beall, Ph.D.
Chairman, Dept. of Old Testament Literature and Exegesis
Capital Bible Seminary
Lanham, MD 20706

"The Secret of Right Relationships by author David Derby does a splendid job of drawing information from a variety of sources. David makes extensive use of his own personal experiences while linking his writing to the global Christian Church as well. His extensive use of Biblical texts draws all of his writing together. It is clear he has a passionate concern for sharing the Good News in small towns as well as in great cities in the United States to Latin America to Africa and India. His message is a universal one that the human soul is 'restless until it finds its rest in God.' You will gain insight by reading his book."

David S. Oyler
General Presbyter
Presbytery of Lake Erie

"I'm delighted to recommend the creative writing of David Derby to help us all overcome dinosaur thinking. David's insights, coming from a lifetime of leadership experiences in business, ministry, and missionary service, can help Christians in leadership roles to recognize the attitudes and actions that hinder us from being effective in our service for Christ. Based firmly on the Bible and filled with practical illustrations, *The Secret of Right Relationships*_will change the way you lead. Read it, enjoy it, and put it into use for the fulfilling of our Leader's Great Commission!"

Dr. Edward Huntley
Pastor, The Federated Church
East Springfield, PA

"We really appreciate Dr. David Derby's ministry of training people using the India edition of this book, *Overcoming Dinosaur Thinking to Receive God's Blessings*. (Dr. is an honorary title we bestowed on him.) We praise God for the anointing Dr. Derby has from the Lord. He teaches Biblical Truths in a most simple way to touch and guide one's heart to realize how he should live so that he would receive the blessings of God. Using the illustrations of dinosaurs' nature and actions and comparing them with man's nature and behavior is not only a new thought to us, but it brought such a deeper meaning which gave us a transparent idea to examine ourselves and our spiritual lives. Most people from our group started to find out their weaknesses, and are now trying to bring those before God Almighty to overcome.

"We understand that God's love is wonderful, and there are graces waiting for us to fill our lives when we give God first place, and forsake our old nature through the power of the Holy Spirit. We learned that we should not live for ourselves, but for God and others. We all are thankful to Dr. Derby for coming from so far with love in action spending his time to teach us about the secrets of right relationships."

Rev. Subrata Sarkar
General Secretary, Covenant Family Churches
Purulia, West Bengal, India

"I have been privileged to partner with David Derby for many years as he has, with excellence and with great zeal, shared the Good News of the Gospel of Jesus Christ both locally and globally. I have met few persons in my lifetime with his calling. His book, *The Secret of Right Relationships* captures the essence of his journey and authentically defines true discipleship."

Harold Ferraro
Senior Pastor, New Beginnings Church of God
Meadville, Pennsylvania

"Provocative and engaging… *The Secret of Right Relationships* challenges the readers to evaluate their paradigms and examine how to improve their relationships from a Biblical perspective. God desires that you have successful, healthy and productive relationships. This book is a practical guide on how to do so."

Bishop Stanley K. Smith,
Pastor, St. John MFGBC, Meadville PA
Pennsylvania State Bishop
Full Gospel Baptist Church Fellowship International

"David Derby is a mission-minded and committed person who lives a simple life style that enabled him to come to India with the Indian edition of this book. His experience, professionalism, and leadership effectiveness are reflected throughout the time proven information on true discipleship presented in this work which is a treasure chest full of insight. Within these pages, you'll find irrefutable wisdom, and David illustrates the secrets of right relationships through interesting real-life stories, and personal anecdotes. The ideas presented are simple, clear, and easy to grasp…yet profound! It is an enjoyable easy-to-read book that is educational, yet entertaining.

"If you want to lead or develop relationships needed for true discipleship, this will be an important book for you."

Pastor Rajesh Patole
Executive Secretary
Association of Christian Alliance of the C&MA, INDIA

"David loves the Lord and the Unreached People of India. He has gone where most Christians would not go. David and his dear wife, Colleen, spend much of their money to do the work of the Lord. I have a special affinity for their work as I am originally from India and have a heart for reaching its Unreached. David has been there several times and has established very good contacts and partnerships with Indian Christian leaders and missionaries. They have caught his compassion and vision to reach the Unreached using his unique training to help indigenous pastors so they will continue what the Lord enabled David to set up.

"Even though David cannot be in India, the Lord actually is multiplying the outreach of his work. May God the Almighty continue to use and help David and Colleen do the work for which they have such a passion."

Nirmal Sarvotham
Field Coordinator for India
Missionary Ventures International

"David Derby has written a volume of creative thinking in this his new monograph. *The Secret of Right Relationship*, subtitled *Overcoming Dinosaur Thinking*, has captured the imagination of a new generation of students of the WORD and psychological thought. Derby's *Compassion* and *Passion* for the millions who do not know joy or peace is compelling.

"Written for persons who have education in theology and psychology as well as those who are reading at or below a sixth grade level, Derby makes plain the basics of discipleship understanding."

Juanita E. Leonard, Ph.D
Anderson University School of Theology
Professor of Christian Mission Emeriti
Anderson, Indiana U S A

"It's our joy that Dr. David Derby came to our midst to teach us about practical Christian behavior using his Indian edition of this book. (Dr. is an honorary title we bestowed on him)

"He has taught us in a very simple manner. We all have learned the great secret to be a good disciple of Jesus Christ. We also have learned how to get rid of fear, anxiety and bitterness through the available power of the Holy Spirit and prayer.

"The seminar has taught us such good lessons which made all of us think a different way. We are now aware of how our lives should be used to glorify God."

Titus Raito
General Secretary, Saura Baptist Christian Mandali Sammiloni
Serango, Orissa, India

"David Derby's study *The Secret of Right Relationships* invites readers to 'become the person God intends for us to be.' To become that person, one must be transformed…one must be able to overcome their present circumstance. This study renews one's mind by reminding us that we were created to live as community rather than live as beings who accomplish little through fragmented efforts. It creates a sense of belonging and provides a structure for learning… learn how to look past negative instincts and tap into the power of gifts, hospitality, and generosity. I'm eagerly looking forward to the possibility that this unique study will be made available for those who need to hear its invitation to discover Hope (Jesus)."

Tom Corcoran
Multi Church D.C.

"David Derby's book and program *The Secret of Right Relationships*, subtitled *Overcoming Dinosaur Thinking* will help your ministry or business move forward with excellence, and it will help you mature in many areas of your life. I had David present a one day leadership seminar and was impressed with everything he shared."

Pastor Dennis See
Director of the Altar International House of Prayer, Meadville
and Pa House of Prayer Network

DEDICATION

My ministry started with my mother's prayers long before I could remember. I was born a hydrocephalic, a condition where the fluid on the brain cannot escape. This condition causes severe retardation, the head to enlarge to several times its normal size, and a short life expectancy. The pressure from the fluid build-up caused headaches, and I cried most of the time. My mother prayed constantly for me when I was a baby, and she dedicated my life to God's service if He would heal me of this condition. I was healed when I was 10 months old.

Fifty-five years later my mother had a stroke. At that time I was scheduled to go to Zambia to field test the first edition of this book. I was going to cancel the trip to be with Mom, but she said, "No! You are to go and do God's work." We prayed together and said our good-byes knowing she might not be alive on this side of Heaven when I returned. She died while I was in Zambia.

I dedicate this book to my mother, Dorothy Mae Derby Frampton, whose love and prayers, guided by the Holy Spirit, gave me the passion to go and make disciples of all nations, not just to the outermost parts of the world, but also to my own.

CONTENTS

FOREWORD

One problem Christendom faces today is indulging in the spiritual delights of religious language without the practice of obedience. Religiosity, without true obedience, produces spiritual hypocrisy and snobbery that is on the increase due to gross negligence of churches and mission organizations to provide proper disciple-making and training. In Matthew 28:19-20, the Master Disciple-Maker and Trainer, Jesus Christ, commissioned His disciples to make disciples of all nations. However, today many churches and mission organizations mainly focus on making believers and baptizing them without laying the foundation of true discipleship. Many indigenous mission organizations even exaggerate the facts and figures to show them being more productive than they actually are—pretending to be what they are not. Jesus Christ sternly warns against such hypocrisy and deceit.

David Derby, a well experienced behavioral consultant, speaker, author and trainer, has a deep passion for training believers to be better disciples of Jesus Christ. *The Secret of Right Relationships: Overcoming Dinosaur Thinking*, hits the nail on the head in saying that dinosaurs have been extinct for a long time, but "dinosaur thinking" remains. This has been the main cause of all kinds of problems and conflicts that humanity, at large, and Christendom, in particular, are facing. "Dinosaur thinking" produces a self-centered, egotistical, and controlling person. Yes, "Dinosaur Thinking" is alien and contrary to the mind of Christ. Selfishness mars our life, our witness, and our ministry. It replaces a Christ-like mind set. St. Paul writes in his epistle to the Philippians:

> *"Do nothing out of selfish ambition or vain conceit. Rather, in humility value others above yourselves, not looking to your own interests but each of you to the interests of others. In your relationships with one another, have the same mindset as Christ Jesus:" Phil 2:3-5.*

David Derby rightly points out that when we follow dinosaur instincts we are prevented from being blessed and from being a blessing to others. This is because Dinosaur Thinkers see the world as being one big pie, and their goal is to grab the biggest piece possible! To be a true disciple of Christ, one must overcome his Dinosaur Thinking.

May the good Lord use Brother David Derby mightily to train people to be better disciples of Jesus Christ.

Rev. Dr. Diamond Philus
General Administrator
MISSION INDIA DEVELOPMENT CENTRE

INTRODUCTION
Why Overcoming Dinosaur Thinking
Is the Theme of This Book?

M y wife, Colleen, and I have been blessed over the years with a wide diversity of experiences as God has guided us in the development of *The Secret of Right Relationships*.

The concept of this study started more than 35 years ago when I was a counselor-house parent at George Junior Republic, a correctional facility in western Pennsylvania for adjudicated delinquent teenage boys. There I studied behavior modification and developed a program to help effectuate positive character change.

I worked there when Colleen and I married. She then moved into my big house with me and my six adjudicated delinquents.

A year later, Colleen and I left the group home so I could attend Gordon-Conwell Theological Seminary. We wanted to follow God's leading to become who He was calling us to be. After a year of seminary, we ran out of money and returned home to Meadville, PA. It was never our intention for me to become an ordained pastor.

Shortly after returning home, the Lord led me to develop a specialized foster parent program for Crawford County in which I provided family counseling to the families of the teenage boys placed in our care. My behavior modification program, where the boys were not given any privileges until they earned them, usually brought about the desired behavior. I counseled the boys' parents about my program and helped them set up similar contingencies. Usually by the third week, our youths would be allowed to return to their homes for the weekends. If they violated any of their parents' new rules, I brought them back to my home with strict consequences. The program normally lasted six months.

Colleen and I phased out this program when our two oldest natural born children, Jeff and Heather, were three and four, and the Lord led me to develop my first workshop entitled, "Help for Parents and Other People Who Work with Their Kids." He opened the door for me to facilitate this training at several churches and at foster parent, caseworker, and school workshops. A parent, who attended one of my workshops, asked if I would give the same type of training at his business. I soon learned that I could make more money facilitating training for businesses than I received from church honorariums.

I joined SPEAKERS USA, a professional speakers association, to hone my facilitation skills. One of its workshops suggested I should develop a theme for my training. The Lord led me to choose "Overcoming Dinosaur Thinking." While developing this theme, I studied instinctive behavior psychology and added some of these concepts to the Biblical principles I was using. As I studied instinctive behavior, I discovered that each of its rules, that in this book I call "dinosaur thinking rules," described a tendency toward sin. I knew a greater understanding of instinctive behavior and how God calls His people to overcome these tendencies would help marriages, and improve parenting, leadership, team building, and conflict resolution skills. This would also help with stress management and character building.

The above benefits fit within the two bookends of my early workshop entitled, "The Secret of Success is Overcoming Dinosaur Brains." The first bookend, which begins our training, is on listening. The dinosaur never listened because he probably had no ears. He had holes on the side of his head so he could hear and react to his environment. But he never listened, because to listen, one must care about the person talking. The dinosaur thinker only cares about himself. The closing bookend is fear of change. "Dinosaur thinking" resists change. I like to think that at the last great council of the dinosaurs they didn't like the pressure to do things differently. So they unanimously voted not to change, and that is why they became extinct.

The Lord blessed us as I became a popular motivational speaker and consultant. It was my goal to help businesses and to encourage Christians in discovering their full potential. God didn't waste any of my life experiences as He used them to enrich our programs.

The Lord led an African evangelist to live with us for five months in 2001. This man had a great love for God and a passion to reach and help the people in his country. As he shared his heart with me, he appreciated my listening. But every time I would disagree with what he said, he would go ballistic. Once he yelled at me saying, "I don't need to understand how Americans think. I just need to tell them of the needs of the people in my country, and they will want to give." Another time he yelled, "How can you be smart enough to understand the situation and at the same time be so stupid as to disagree with me?" He knew I understood what he said, but he saw no need to try to understand why I might disagree. I knew he would not accomplish his fund raising goal without developing better people skills. Then it occurred to me that my book might help him. I left a copy of "The Secret of Success Is Overcoming Dinosaur Brains" on the kitchen table for him to find.

The next day, he asked me, "What is this?" I told him it was a leadership training workbook.

He said, "I never had any training in leadership. This might be good for me."

We left the next day for two weeks of visiting churches and Christian colleges. He read the workbook to me, and we discussed it as I drove. I also gave him a hand-out on developing listening skills. I had him practice listening to me as to why I disagreed with him in some areas. At first it was difficult for him not to tell me why I was wrong, but he finally understood the object of listening was to thoroughly understand what a person thought and felt. He realized for the first time that a person could understand a position without agreeing with it. Once he understood why I had disagreed, and was willing to work through our differences, we were able to work together, and he raised more money for his project in the next two weeks than he had in the prior six months.

With his encouragement, I rewrote the book, adding a Bible study to each chapter. We field tested that first edition when I went to in Zambia in 2005. I praise God for this latest edition, *The Secret of Right Relationships*. At the time of this printing, it has been translated into six languages.

We see excitement in people in America, Africa, and Asia who have attended the seminar this book is based on. Many say it has changed their lives and want to share it with others. We use a "train the trainer" model and encourage those who take the training to use this book as a teacher's guide to teach others. We take the old Chinese proverb: Give a man a fish and he will eat for a day. Teach a man to fish and he will eat for a lifetime. We expand it to: Train a teacher to teach people how to fish and you save a village. Train leaders to train teachers to teach people how to fish and you can save a nation.

Many Americans have told me they have read this book to their children. Many of the Grass Roots Church Planters, GRCP, in India have taught it in their house churches and/or have their own training workshops to teach it to other GRCP and their church leaders.

We pray it will also bless you.

PREFACE

My first memory of seeing "dinosaur thinking" was back in 1958 as I was sitting beside Charlie, my big brother, on a warm sunny day. Four or five other neighborhood kids sat with us on the small bridge in the middle of Carlton, Pennsylvania. We entertained ourselves by naming the year, make, and model of the occasional cars that passed by.

Splash! All of us got wet as Bob and Bill, visiting cousins of one of our neighbors, threw a bucket of creek water up over the bridge. Charlie threatened to rearrange their body parts if they did it again.

A few minutes later, our eyes focused on a brand new red Chevrolet convertible. Unknown to us, Bob had another bucket of water, and Bill waited beside the bridge to give the signal.

"Now!" Bill yelled, and Bob threw the water. The driver slammed on the brakes as Bill and Bob ran for some high grass a few yards away. The couple in the car were soaked. We were stunned as the lady passenger ran toward us. She grabbed Charlie by the shirt with one hand, and with the other slapped him three or four times across his face. She yelled, "How dare you throw water on us. This is our first drive in our new car, and you ruined it!"

"But Ma'am, I didn't do it!" Charlie said.

"You didn't do it? I saw you! How dare you lie to me when I caught you red-handed!" she said as she started slapping him again.

I yelled, "Stop hitting him. He didn't do it!"

She stopped, looked over the side of the bridge, and saw the bucket Bob had left. She did not hear Bob and Bill laughing in the high grass. "There's the bucket you threw over the bridge when you saw me coming!" She started slapping Charlie a third time as she yelled, "How dare you lie to me. I saw you! You liar!"

Her husband restrained her. He said, "Let's get out of here," and they left.

I often remember this incident. How could that lady have been so certain she saw Charlie throw the water? And then I remember when I've acted just as crazy as that lady and blamed someone for doing something only to discover later I was wrong. As Christians, we should be able to control ourselves. Scripture says, *"If anyone is in Christ, he is a new creation; the old has gone and the new has come." (2 Corinthians 5:17)* But there are times, *"I do not understand what I do. For what I want to do I do not do, but what I hate, I do." (Romans 7:15)*

We are created in God's image, and the best word to describe His image is love. God's entire law is summed up in a single command: *"Love your neighbor as yourself." (Galatians 5:14)* When we live by the Spirit of God's law we will produce the fruit of the Spirit: *"love, joy, peace, patience, kindness, goodness, faithfulness gentleness and self-control. Against such things there is no law." (Galatians 5:22b-23)*

However, we are born with a sinful nature that displays *"hatred, discord, jealousy, fits of rage, selfish ambition, dissensions, factions and envy." (Galatians 5:20a)* This sinful nature, that I call "dinosaur thinking," will lead to death and destruction if not overcome by God's grace through the blood of Jesus.

Dinosaurs were ancient animals. Some grew to be larger than elephants with necks longer than giraffes and tails longer than crocodiles. But these animals had brains no bigger than a chicken's brain. They did not think. Their brain was only large enough to provide them with instincts to gratify their wants, to fear the unknown, and to avoid danger. Dinosaurs have been extinct for a long time, but "dinosaur thinking" remains. It compels us to want to dominate others, act defensively, and avoid accepting responsibility. Today's dinosaur thinkers never follow through on what they started yesterday, but do what is fun, easy, and provides instant gratification. When we follow the instincts of our "dinosaur thinking" we have predictable outcomes of behaviors that prevent us from developing constructive and affirmative relationships.

I have a heart to train Christians world-wide so they can in turn train others. My goal in writing this American edition is to help American Christians become better disciples, and Lord willing through the sales of this book, plus honorariums and speaker fees, raise funds to underwrite the cost to translate the Indian edition into several more languages. We also pray to subsidize the cost for native

Indian missionaries to continue to provide this discipleship training to Grass Roots Church Planters.

My prayer for you is that God uses this book to help you learn how to make better relationships by enabling you to overcome your "dinosaur thinking" and avoid triggering it in others. By so doing, God will bless you, and He will be glorified as you pass His blessings on to others.

Chapter One
DOMINATION
(I'm The Boss)—Part One

This Chapter Deals
With Our Sinful Nature of
Wanting to Control Others

The person trapped in "dinosaur thinking" is compelled to have the last word during arguments because that makes him feel dominant. He is the winner! When dinosaurs roamed the earth, the losers of confrontations were often eaten. Today, the loser of an argument may return to get even.

A dinosaur thinker cannot be challenged by differing ideas or opinions and cannot allow disagreement. If he hears an opposing idea, he is quick to point out how it is in error. He demands control of the conversation. He feels it is okay to interrupt you, but refuses to allow you to interrupt him. He will not obey the Scriptural admonition to *"be quick to listen, slow to speak, and slow to become angry." (James 1:19)*

My rule is:
You are **not** allowed to interrupt me.
But I can interrupt you whenever I want.

To truly listen, we must put aside our defenses and differences and care about the person talking. We must resist the temptation to interrupt. Many conversations are just monologues in duet. Are you really listening as you wait for a pause and think about your responses to the person talking? Scripture says, *"He who answers before listening—that is his folly and his shame,"* *(Proverbs 18:13)*

Sometimes we find ourselves in an undesirable argument. We get louder and louder, speak faster and faster, and we wonder how we got sucked into such a waste of time. After all, 'He will never see it my way!' The dinosaur thinker doesn't use logic or allow others to have an opinion. He doesn't care about feelings. The only thing the dinosaur thinker understands is, 'If I have the last word, I WIN!'

Jesus never argued. He simply spoke the truth in love. He told the rich young man, *"If you want to be perfect, go, sell your possessions and give to the poor, and you will have treasure in heaven." (Matt: 19:21)* Jesus allowed him to walk away without further comment. Jesus didn't brow beat him or try to yell him into submission. He let him make his own decision.

You can quickly end most arguments by saying, "I'm sorry." You aren't admitting you're wrong. It is showing you are more concerned about that person and your relationship than being right. 'I'm sorry' is difficult to say when you're angry. You can often end the argument by shutting your mouth and letting the other person have the last word. This may be especially wise when communicating with a hard-headed dinosaur that is trying to yell you into submission and perceives saying "I'm sorry" as admitting fault.

Ouch

Once when I was hanging a picture, I missed the nail and hit my thumb with the hammer. I yelled something that you would not expect a Christian to say. To which my wife said, "It's not my fault!"

I yelled, "I know it is not your fault! I'm the dummy who hit my thumb with the hammer."

She said, "You don't need to get mad at me."

I said, "I'm not mad at you. Can't I yell because it hurts and I'm mad at myself?"

Again she said, "Well, you don't need to get upset!"

I said, "You know this stupid argument could have been avoided if instead of saying, "It's not my fault!" you could have simply said, "I'm sorry."

Squabbling Siblings

It's also difficult to stop two dinosaur thinkers in an argument. Once when I was pastoring, I was called to the kitchen phone just as my two older children were starting dishes. Back then we did not have cordless or cell phones. The kitchen phone had a stretchy coil line connecting the receiver to the phone on the wall. Because of this, I couldn't leave the kitchen to go to a quiet area. A church member told me her husband had just died of a heart attack. I asked my children to be quiet, as they were beginning to argue about whose turn it was to wash and dry. Then I heard the call waiting tone. It was the lady's daughter-in-law. Her son had also died in another hospital from complications of a long illness. I ordered my children to stop arguing. But because their "dinosaur thinking" was engaged, they were unwilling to stop and even grew louder. I had to hang up the phone to get their attention.

Feisty Old Dinosaur

The following story illustrates that sometimes what a dinosaur thinker perceives in an argument is far from reality. One day I heard a commotion at the intersection up the street from my group home where I was a counselor-house parent for delinquent teenage boys. The mother of Roy, one of my boys, had gotten confused and turned the wrong way on a one-way street as she was returning Roy from a two week home visit. A young man in another car blew his horn. Roy's father jumped out of the car cussing, swearing, shaking his cane at the young man, and yelling, "Come out of that car, you punk. I'm going to teach you a lesson."

Roy's mother pleaded with her husband to get back into the car because she was afraid he would have another stroke or heart attack.

A policeman arrived at the same time I did. The feisty old man instantly started daring the officer to arrest him. The officer, seeing that I knew him, let me handle the situation. A couple of my other boys helped Roy take his father to the house. Roy's mother was in tears. We got her settled down, and the officer directed traffic as I turned the car around and drove Roy's mother to the house.

Roy's father said, "I really feel good. It's been a long time since I've been in a good scrap. Mr. Derby, we make a great team. We really taught that punk kid a lesson didn't we? And the cop! He backed down when he saw you. He knew not to mess with you!"

We see similar "dinosaur thinking" when people position themselves to become the most important. We see this with the disciples when they argued among themselves as to who would be the greatest. (See Luke 9:46) It is sometimes seen when leaders of various organizations are overly protective of their position and want the plans for programs to go through them. This may prevent members from maturing in leadership. Sometimes when a church sees another church starting a new ministry, it starts its own competing ministry instead of combining forces to show a unified Christian witness. We can get much more done if we overcome our "dinosaur thinking" and only care about God getting the credit and glory, and not be concerned about any earthly gratification for ourselves.

"Domination dinosaur thinking" can lead to unethical behavior. This is sometimes seen in government, businesses, and ministries when people manipulate others to gain control. They don't respect the people under their authority and see nothing wrong with manipulating funds to their pet projects or for their personal gain. You see it with people who require you to give them a bribe to provide you with a service to which you are entitled or have already paid. Dinosaur thinkers see life as being one pie, and their goal is to get the biggest piece possible. To get a bigger piece, they feel others must get a smaller piece.

Pastors' Argument

One time when I was in Africa, two pastors fought over which of their churches I would be preaching at on Sunday morning. When I was asked to decide, they reluctantly agreed that I could be with both because one met at 9 and the other at 11. I was amazed when the pastor of the first church prayed, "Our Father who brought this servant from America to help us meet our financial needs." He forgot what I taught in *Overcoming Dinosaur Thinking* ("I Want It Now!" and "Get the Mate.") You will learn about these rules in future chapters.

I used this story as an illustration in a later workshop. Some attendees told me of an incident where a delegation from a church killed some people from another church so they could be the first to meet a short-term American missionary team at the airport.

Onward Christian Soldiers

An unfortunate illustration of "domination dinosaur thinking" occurred in a church between its first woman pastor and the church's male choir director of more than 25 years. They disagreed on many issues. One was that the director insisted that old hymns like "Onward Christian Soldiers" be sung during worship. The pastor wanted him to teach the new hymns she had chosen from the new denominational hymnal. She showed him in her denominational Book of Order that the pastor had the final say in what would be sung. She even asked the district supervisor to support her position.

The following Sunday the choir sang a special rendition of "Onward Christian Soldiers." After the service the pastor and the choir director had a screaming argument. The next day the pastor marched triumphantly into the district office and announced, "The conflict is resolved. He left the church!" The next Sunday, she discovered that 80 percent of the church's members left with him.

Question 1: (for discussion)

Can a person who always has to have the last word, who treats others as inferior, or manipulates others to gain control, be a good leader? Can he be a good disciple of Jesus Christ? Will he have good relationships?

"My dear brothers, take note of this: Everyone should be quick to listen, slow to speak and slow to become angry."(James 1:19)

Jesus said, "You know that the rulers of the Gentiles lord it over them, and their high officials exercise authority over them. Not so with you. Instead, whoever wants to become great among you must be your servant, and whoever wants to be first must be your slave– just as the Son of Man did not come to be served, but to serve, and to give his life as a ransom for many." (Matthew 20:25-28)

Question 2:

What examples of "domination dinosaur thinking" have you observed?

Some examples could be:

Dinosaur thinkers love to get revenge. That is why there are so many movies in which the hero avenges himself by killing people who have done him or someone in his family wrong. Have you ever fantasized about telling off someone or getting revenge? If you have, you know first-hand what "domination dinosaur thinking" is.

Have you ever said, "Can't you see I'm busy?" to a spouse or child who comes to you to ask for something? This is "dinosaur thinking." You are communicating, "I'm more important than you." or "What I'm doing is of greater value than anything you could want." Yelling at your spouse or child when you are busy doesn't show a good Christian example. Nor does it help you. It is hard to work when you are angry, and you may get more interruptions from an upset spouse or a pouting child. It is a good Christian example to give your spouse or child some attention and to return to your work with everyone happy.

Question 3:

What examples of "domination dinosaur thinking" or (I'm the boss! thinking) have you seen in yourself? How has this impacted your relationships?

An example that I sometimes see in myself is becoming upset with my wife when I can't find something. I'll blame her for losing something or putting something away so I can't find it. Often I later discover where I put it. Getting angry prevents us from thinking clearly.

Smoking Swirly

Once back in the 60's (when I was in high school and before I accepted Jesus) my instinctive "dinosaur thinking" was triggered. Some students enjoyed sneaking a smoke in the restrooms. They would stand at the urinal as if they were doing their business and smoke their cigarette. As soon as they would see the restroom door open, they would put their cigarette in front of them. If a teacher came in to check the restroom, the smoker would flick the cigarette into the urinal and flush it. But if it were a student, he would put the cigarette back in his mouth.

One day as I entered the restroom, I used the urinal beside a smoker. He took a big drag, and blew the smoke in my face. Without thinking, I shoved his head into the urinal and flushed it. I wonder what he would think after all of these years to learn that the jock who gave him a swirly became a pastor and missionary.

"Domination dinosaur thinking" is man's natural tendency for self-gratification. Scripture says,

> *"Therefore as God's chosen people, holy and dearly loved, clothe yourselves with compassion, kindness, humility, gentleness, and patience. Bear with each other and forgive whatever grievances you may have against one another. Forgive as the Lord forgave you." (Colossians 3:12-13)*

Question 4:
What does God mean by clothe yourself with kindness?

_____

_____

_____

Many Christians don't practice kindness. Clothing yourself with kindness or putting on kindness is something you must decide to do.

> *"Love is patient, love is kind." (1 Corinthians 13:4a) and, "Be kind and compassionate to one another, forgiving each other, just as in Christ God forgave you. (Ephesians 4:32)*

Question 5:
What is the difference between being kind and doing kind things?

_____

_____

_____

_____

_____

We are used to doing and not being. Usually we are kind when others are kind to us. That is doing kindness. But being kind is being kind even to people who are not kind to you. Your "dinosaur thinking" is scared of kindness and is afraid that someone may take advantage of you. God wants to be glorified, and He is glorified when by faith you allow His kindness to be inside of you. God wants us to overcome our "dinosaur thinking" with kindness.

> *His divine power has given us everything we need for life and godliness through our knowledge of Him who called us by his own glory and goodness. Through these he has given us his very great and precious promises, so that through them you may participate in the divine nature and escape the corruption in the world caused by evil desires.*

For this very reason, make every effort to add to your faith goodness; and to goodness, knowledge; and to knowledge, self-control; and to self-control, perseverance; and to perseverance, godliness; and to godliness, brotherly kindness; and to brotherly kindness, love. For if you possess these qualities in increasing measure they will keep you from being ineffective and unproductive in your knowledge of our Lord Jesus Christ. But if anyone does not have them, he is nearsighted and blind, and has forgotten that he has been cleansed from his past sins. (2 Peter 1:3-9)

Bad Day

When our son, Jeff, was in 2nd grade his speech teacher sent a scathing three-page letter home with him. She was disappointed with his progress and blamed his mother and me for not doing a long list of things to help him. I wrote on the top of her note, "WOW! You must have had a bad day. We are working at home with Jeff one hour each evening." The next day she sent home a short note in which she wrote, "I did have a bad day. You are doing enough. Thanks!"

Question 6: (for discussion)

What would have happened if I had written back a scathing three-page letter questioning her abilities as a teacher? Or what would have happened if I had taken the letter to her principal and complained?

"And without faith it is impossible to please God, because anyone who comes to Him must believe that He exists and that He rewards those who earnestly seek him. (Hebrews 11:6) and "In the same way, faith by itself, if not accompanied by action, is dead." (James 2:17)

Question 7: (for discussion)
Can faith grow by only reading the Bible and praying?

Some people think so. You need to read your Bible and pray. But you also need to put your faith in action in order for it to really grow. One way to put your faith in action is to practice kindness. Many Christians don't practice kindness. Learning to be kind is like learning to ride a bicycle. You can read all you want about bikes and other people who have ridden them, but you are not going to learn how until you climb on and start pedaling.

Reflections

"But love your enemies, do good to them, and lend to them without expecting to get anything back. Then your reward will be great, and you will be sons of the Most High, because he is kind to the ungrateful and wicked. Be merciful, just as your Father is merciful." (Luke 6:35)

Jesus says, "A new commandment I give you: Love one another. As I have loved you, so you must love one another. All men will know that you are my disciples if you love one another." (John 13:34-35)

"There is no limit to what can be accomplished if it doesn't matter who gets the credit." *Ralph Waldo Emerson*

"We need to learn how to agree to disagree and get on with the basic living out of the Christian Life." *George Verwer*

"Conversation is a competitive exercise in which the person who draws the first breath is declared the listener." *Suzette Haden Elgin*

Do not merely listen to the Word, and so deceive yourselves. Do what is says. (James 1:22)

Chapter Two
DOMINATION
(I'm The Boss)—Part Two

2

America's First Encounter with Islam

Photograph from London Times[1]

Prior to America's Revolutionary War, American merchant ships sailing through the Mediterranean Sea were protected by the British Navy from the Barbary Pirates. During and for a short time after the Revolutionary War, American merchant ships depended on the French Navy for protection. The French, however, were unable to provide much help because they were at war with England. They had their own merchant ships to protect. As a result, Barbary Pirates captured American merchant ships, stole the cargo, and sold American seamen into slavery.

In 1786, Thomas Jefferson and John Adams negotiated with Tripoli's envoy to London, Ambassador Sidi Haji Abdrahaman or (Sidi Haji Abdul Rahman Adja). They asked him by what right he extorted money and took slaves.

The ambassador answered that the right was founded on the Laws of the Prophet (Mohammed). It was written in the Quran that all nations who did not answer to their authority were sinners, and it was their right and duty to make war upon sinners wherever they could be found. They were to make slaves of everyone they took as prisoners. Every Mussulman (or Muslim) who should be slain in battle was sure to go to paradise. [2]

The ambassador referred to the following two verses in the Quran: *"And fight them until there is no more Fitnah (disbelief and polytheism: i.e. worshipping others besides Allah) and the religion (worship) will all be for Allah alone (in the whole of the world)." (Sura 8:39)*, and *"Jihad (holy fighting in Allah's Cause) is ordained for you (Muslims)" (Sura 2:216a)*

Modern World Tensions

In our modern world, the average everyday Muslim is not a theologian, a terrorist, an extremist, or a devout religious person. However, there are bands of Muslim extremists who feel it is their destiny to rule the world. These groups believe it is acceptable to use terrorism to accomplish their goals. The chaos they are creating is the result of unchecked "dinosaur thinking."

Many people throughout the world think evangelical Christians also want to rule the world. But Jesus does not call us to rule the world. He calls us to make Him known to every people group. His love transcends languages, cultures, and political and economic systems.

Ask an average group of Christians, "What is your basic belief?" Most likely their answer will be, "If we confess our sins and accept Jesus as Lord we will go to Heaven when we die." Ask an average group of Muslims the same question, "What is your basic belief?" Most likely they will say, "One day Islam will dominate the world." With the exception of dying in a Jihad, there is no assurance in Islam that a good Muslim will go to Heaven (Paradise) when he dies. A good Muslim could follow all of the laws of Islam and not go to Paradise because Islam teaches that Allah can change his mind.

God wants us to overcome our "dinosaur thinking" of wanting to be dominant. He wants us to love Him with all of our mind, heart, and soul, and He wants us to love our neighbor as ourselves. This includes our neighbors around the world who hate us. Yes, our nation must defend itself against terrorism. But we must live lives that will model God's love. And we must pray as Jesus taught His disciples to pray, that God's Kingdom come on earth as it is in Heaven. This is not pushing our political or economic systems or our culture. And we are certainly not called to be terrorists. The Christian mission is sharing that there is a void in all men's lives which only Jesus Christ can fill.

Question 1:

What was God's first command for mankind?

God's first command to all of mankind was for humans to spread out and populate the earth. (Genesis 1:28) Over centuries of time this would result in cultural diversities of language, food, clothing, and more.

> *"Then God blessed Noah and his sons, saying to them, 'Be fruitful and increase in number and fill the earth.'" Genesis 9:1* and *"As for you, be fruitful and increase in number, multiply on the earth and increase upon it." (Genesis 9:7)*

The Tower of Babel

Now the whole world had one language and a common speech. As men moved eastward, they found a plain in Shinar and settled there.

They said to each other, "Come, let's make bricks and bake them thoroughly." They used brick instead of stone, and tar instead of mortar. Then they said, "Come, let us build ourselves a city, with a tower that reaches to the heavens, so that we may make a name for ourselves and not be scattered over the face of the whole earth."

But the Lord came down to see the city and the tower that the men were building. The Lord said, "If as one people speaking the same language they have begun to do this, then nothing they plan will be impossible for them. Come, let us go down and confuse their language so they will not understand each other." So the Lord scattered them from there over all the earth. (Genesis 11:1-8a)

Question 2: (for discussion)

Why did the people of Babel say, "Come, let us build ourselves a city, with a tower that reaches to the heavens, so that we may make a name for ourselves and not be scattered over the face of the whole earth."?

_____

_____

_____

_____

Their "dinosaur thinking" caused them to ignore God's instructions. They wanted to be dominant over God, self-reliant, and to protect themselves in case of another flood. They were afraid to move out of their comfort zone.

God loves diversity and to be worshipped by believers in all languages and cultures. Because God loves diversity among His people, He divided the people of the world into about 70 people groups through the destruction of the Tower of Babel and the scattering of the people all over the earth.

Indigenous Languages of Mexico

The following story of migrant Indian farm workers in Mexico is a relatively recent historical example of a Babel-like scattering of people.

Each year thousands of Native Americans (Indians) migrate from their homes in southern Mexico to harvest crops in the north. While strongly resistant to the Gospel in their tribal areas, they are receptive when they hear the message in the work camps.

Most American Christians think that the only language a missionary needs in Mexico is Spanish. They are not aware of the anthropological ramifications from Mexican history. The Aztecs, a Native American tribe, had already conquered all of the other indigenous tribes of Mexico when the Spanish explorers arrived in the early 1500's. Because the Spaniards had white skin and guns, and could perform trickery with their advanced technology, the Aztecs thought the Spanish were gods. It was relatively easy for the Spanish to conquer them and thus gain control of all of Mexico. Hundreds of thousands were forced into slavery or killed. Millions of Indians died from hardship and disease, and their population became smaller. As male soldiers and explorers continued to come from Spain, they intermarried with native women. This growing population of "Mestizos", with mixed European and Native American blood, spoke Spanish as their primary language. They make up close to ninety percent of Mexico's population today. But the ten percent who managed to survive scattered, never to return to their original tribal group. Thus, the few people groups from 500 years ago have diversified into groups that speak more than 300 languages and dialects today.

The Call of Abram

Now notice God's calling of Abram that immediately follows the story of the Tower of Babel.

> *The Lord had said to Abram, "Leave your country, your people and your father's household and go to the land I will show you. "I will make you into a great nation and I will bless you; I will make your name great, and you will be a blessing. I will bless those who bless you, and whoever curses you, I will curse; and all peoples on the earth will be blessed through you." (Genesis 12:1-3)*

Question 3:

Scripture says the Lord told Abram, *"I will make you into a great nation and I will bless you;"* (Genesis 12:2) Do you think this means God loves Abraham's descendants more than all of the other nations, or that God chose them for a special task?

_____

_____

_____

_____

Question 4:

God blessed the nation of Israel to be a blessing. *"And all families on earth will be blessed through you."* (Genesis 12:3b) However, from the very beginning, Israel often disobeyed God and over time they stopped being a blessing to others. How are Christians blessed today through the blessing God gave Abraham?

_____

_____

_____

_____

First of all, we are blessed with Jesus Christ who is the Promised Seed of Abraham. Secondly, God chose to reveal Himself to the Jews and through their experiences with Him we have the Old Testament.

Question 5: (for discussion)

Today the Christian church has the charge to be a blessing by taking the Gospel to all people. What do you think will happen to our blessings of prosperity and freedom if we only see them as our blessings, and don't use them to bless others?

Reflections

But you will receive power when the Holy Spirit comes on you; and you will be my witnesses in Jerusalem, and in all Judea and Samaria, and to the ends of the earth." (Acts 1:8)

"From the stories of others who have become involved in mission work, we learn that the initial inner urgings often seem very subtle, hard to discern. In fact, for most of us, the message really doesn't become clear until we act. It is the process of taking action in response to the Holy Spirit's urging that often provides the real clarity. Without responding, you'll probably never know." *Tetsunao Yamamori*

When God calls or commissions a person, His instructions start with "COME" or "GO:"

> *"Come, follow me," Jesus said, "and I will make you fishers of men." (Matthew 4:19)*

> *Then Jesus came to them and said, "All authority in heaven and on earth has been given to me. Therefore go and make disciples of all nations, baptizing them in the name of the Father and of the Son and of the Holy Spirit, and teaching them to obey everything I have commanded you. And surely I am with you always, to the very end of the age." (Matthew 28:18-20)*

> "Come to me, all you who are weary and burdened, and I will give you rest." (Matthew 11:28)

Chapter Three
TERRITORIALISM
(It's Mine!)

Our Sinful Nature of Selfishness is Revealed

Young children are good examples of "dinosaur territorialism thinking." When another child picks up their toy, they yell, "It's mine!" We try to teach our children to share. But because of Adam's sin, they, as all of mankind, are born with "dinosaur thinking," which tells us to defend our territory.

The following stories show examples of "dinosaur territorialism thinking."

My Seat

One summer when I was in college, I worked night shift at a foundry. My first night I sat at the first available chair in the lunchroom. A few minutes later, a man entered, looked at me, and started ranting and raving. I asked the person next to me if he was always like that.

I was told, "You are sitting in his chair."

I jumped up, "I'm sorry. I didn't realize we had assigned seats."

The man kicked the chair across the room, pushed me up against the wall, and yelled into my face. I can't write what he said, but an acceptable interpretation would be I was a punk kid, I was not to sit in his chair again, and he didn't like me making jokes about assigned seats.

Anger over a lunchroom chair may seem an overreaction. But, it is serious business to a person caught in "dinosaur thinking" and so compelled to defend his territory. You can check out this rule at church on Sunday. You know where certain people always sit. Go early and be sitting in their seats when they arrive. Sometimes you won't know a Christian by his love when you violate what he perceives as his territory.

My Jello

The Jones family experienced "dinosaur territorialism thinking" at their first and last dinner at a church they attended when they moved into town. Mrs. Jones made her special salad of three kinds of cubed Jello mixed with Cool Whip. Everyone at their former church had raved over it. An evening program preceded the dinner, and as it was ending, Mrs. Jones slipped out to help in the kitchen.

As she entered, she saw the matriarch, a long time female member who took charge of everything, dumping her Jello into the garbage disposal.

Mrs. Jones screamed, "That's my Jello salad!"

The matriarch said, "Honey, in this church we use only real whipped cream." Then she hit the disposal switch.

Mrs. Jones cried. The scene attracted a crowd. The matriarch felt justified. Real whipped cream had been a church tradition, and she had to defend it.

My Baby!

A strange example of "dinosaur territorialism thinking" once happened to a couple with a new baby the first Sunday they left the baby in the nursery of their church. The lady doing nursery duty said to the mother, "Don't worry about your baby, if she fusses, I'll nurse her for you."

The mother said, "I don't know about that. I brought a bottle." But, she did not specifically say, "Do not breast feed my baby."

The mother snuck out of worship during the last hymn to see how her baby was doing. She found her being breast fed by the lady in the nursery, and screamed, "She's my baby!" as she grabbed her up into her arms.

The Survey Says

Sometimes a Christian "dinosaur thinking" organization won't change its mind. Many suffer from what I call "committee constipation" and "paralysis by analysis." It takes them a long time to make a decision and when made, it can't be changed.

A former pastor, who also had been a college president, moved down south after retiring. A few years later, he met with the committee of his denomination in charge of planting new churches. He told them that he had always wanted to plant a church, but had been too busy during his professional life as a pastor, professor, and college administrator. After retiring and moving south, he and his wife soon tired of reading and playing shuffleboard, and decided to plant a church. They started with an outreach to their new neighborhood and invited people to a Bible study in their home. They believed in disciple-making, where they shared the love of Christ, taught the Bible, and trained and encouraged their people to reach out and start new Bible studies of their own. Soon the Bible study multiplied, and they rented an elementary school's cafeteria on Sunday so the people from all of the Bible studies could meet for worship and fellowship. The average attendance had grown to 110, and the retired pastor and his wife felt it was time for the congregation to become directly affiliated with their denomination.

The committee chairperson thanked him for his desire to plant a new church. However, the committee had just finished a survey of the churches and the people living in the area and determined that it would be at least ten years before his area would be able to support a new church.

The retired college president told the committee he didn't know how they came to their conclusion. But contrary to their findings, he had planted a new church and wasn't asking for permission to do so or for financial help. He explained that he was an ordained pastor of the denomination and planned to continue as pastor for three more years at no salary. He then informed the committee that the new church planned to purchase property and had consulted with an architect to design plans for a facility that would seat 300. As a retired college president, he had years of experience in fund-raising and would not need money from the denomination. He projected that the church would have a new debt-free building within three years and be fully self-supporting and able to call a younger pastor to continue the ministry. He emphasized that he felt the church should become affiliated with the denomination of which he had always been a member.

He received a letter from the committee the following week. They praised him for his desire to plant a new church. Then they rejected his proposal based on the conclusion of their survey. He then left the denomination and accepted an offer to join another that was happy to receive him and the new church.

Christians Not Welcome

In 2010 my indigenous missionary team and I were the target of "dinosaur thinking" when we arrived at a government guest house deep in a mountain jungle village of Orissa, India. We had a room booked for the night. The guest house attendant apologized stating that the government officials refused to give us the room. The attendant said he wanted to help us, but the officials didn't like Christians, and it didn't matter that we had a reservation; they had the authority to deny us the room. (Extremist Hindu groups from this part of India have a saying, "All white men are Christians; their goal is to evangelize the world; and, they do nothing but make problems for us.")

The attendant told us he might be able to give us a room if we came back after the last official left at 10 PM. When we returned he gave us a room for the night, but we had to be out by 7 AM in order for him to clean it so the officials would not know we had been there. If what the attendant said was true, this is an illustration of a combination of "dinosaur domination and territorialism thinking." The officials were in control and the rooms were theirs to do with as they wanted. On the other hand, the attendant might have been shrewd and simply made up the story so he could pocket the money we paid. In this case, "domination dinosaur thinking" was used to manipulate the system for his gain.

Overcoming Territorialism

I met Santi and Prem, who both pastor about 200 families in their tribal villages, at a seminar I was leading in the mountains of Orissa, India. They left their villages at 6 AM the day before and walked for six hours and then caught a bus to our location. I was the first white man they had ever seen. They said, "We are excited to learn from you because we have heard that you have great teachings."

Santi and Prem planted their churches 20 years ago and had gone through persecution in the early days of their ministries. They said there had been much drinking and poor life choices in their villages prior to them coming to Jesus Christ. "Dinosaur territorialism thinking" in Hindu businessmen caused them to complain to authorities that Christianity was bad for business because Christian converts were not buying alcohol, incense, and the shrines and trinkets to worship gods and goddesses to celebrate Hindu holidays. Police harassed them as their churches were growing. But now the entire village is Christian, and they have peace.

Santi and Prem were excited to return to their villages after the training to share what they had learned. They thanked me for my workbook, *Overcoming Dinosaur Thinking to Receive God's Blessings* that was translated into Oriya, their state's trade language. They planned to use it as a textbook to teach it to the members of their churches and to give seminars to pastors of other villages so they could also learn and teach it.

David with Santi and Prem,
pastors of mountain jungle village churches in Orissa, India

One of my interpreters at a village workshop in Orissa had some bruises and stitches on his head. He said he was preaching the week before in one of the villages when some radical Hindus beat him.

Many of the grass roots church planting pastors who attended our seminars have endured persecution from Hindu extremists under the control of "dinosaur territorialism and domination thinking." We praise God that He opened the doors for us to be able to use the Indian edition of this book to teach Christian leadership and character education to some of His servants on the front lines of the expansion of the Good News of Jesus Christ.

The local grass roots level church planters are encouraged by our caring enough to come to them. Most of them have never been farther than 50 miles away from where they were born. Many walked six hours or more to get to one of the centrally located villages where we had the seminars. Praise God that this training continues throughout remote villages in India even though I've been banned from returning to the country.

A Biblical Illustration

"The crowds were amazed at Jesus' teaching because he taught as one who had authority, and not as their teachers of the law." **(Matthew 7:28b-29a)**

The leaders were jealous because Jesus was encroaching on what they perceived as their territory. They watched Jesus closely, hoping to catch Him breaking the law, and attempted to trap Him in compromising positions. The leaders were always embarrassed when Jesus exposed their schemes. Finally, they plotted to kill Him. (See Mark 12:13-17 and John 11:45-57.)

Question 1:

What examples of "dinosaur territorialism thinking" have you observed? Have you seen it in your own actions?

_____

_____

_____

_____

Here are two examples of "dinosaur territorialism thinking" that I've seen. At one of our workshops in a jungle village in Orissa, India, just as the attendees were having trouble thinking of an example of "territorialism," a young rooster entered the room. He started making advances toward a hen. An old rooster attacked the young rooster. That was chicken talk for, "She is mine!"

 I was proud of myself when I returned from six weeks of facilitating *Overcoming Dinosaur Thinking* seminars in Zambia in 2005. I had gone six weeks without getting irritated. I shared this with my wife over supper the day after returning home. I wondered how long I could continue. After supper, I reclined in my easy chair and started to watch the news. Soon Colleen snuck in and gently removed the remote from my hand.

I said, "I'm watching the news."

Colleen said, "No, you aren't. Your eyes are closed."

I said, "Okay, I'm listening to the news. I don't need to have my eyes open to watch a talking head."

She said, "Well, you are not watching the news, and I want to watch something else." She changed the channel.

I yelled, "Give me that remote!"

How America Became Number One

Most American Christians expect a high standard of living and have no idea how well off they are compared to the rest of the world. How did the USA get this way?

America was in a blessed global position after World War I. The factories of most of the industrialized world had been destroyed, and they looked to the USA to sell them much of what they needed to rebuild. Thus, the American economy boomed, and most of its working people were better off than ever before.

However, greed, which is part of "I want it now dinosaur thinking" that we will study in the next chapter, consumed many Americans. People wanted to get rich, and the rich wanted to get richer. Many invested in the stock market which wasn't well regulated at the time. A person could buy $100 worth of a stock for 10% down and sign a promissory note that he would pay the remaining 90% on demand. He could then leverage that $100 worth of stock as 10% down on another stock worth $1,000. He could then leverage that $1,000 worth of stock for 10% down on another stock worth $10,000. Thus, he could own $11,100 worth of stock with an investment of $10. All went well as long as the stock market kept rising. But the market crashed in October of 1929.

The USA was devastated for the next ten or twelve years. Eventually World War II helped bring us out of The Great Depression. At the end of WWII we were in a similar position as at the end of WWI. Our factories were intact, and the rest of the world had to buy from us to rebuild theirs. Unions became strong because they could demand almost anything they wanted. Management didn't care because they could pass the cost of higher wages and benefits on to its customers. Americans became used to a higher standard of living than the rest of the world. But now, two and three generations later, the rest of the world's factories have been rebuilt, and much of the Third World has entered the industrial age.

Today the USA has stiff competition. But many American Christians feel it is their right to spend an exorbitant amount of money on themselves. After all, why can't we have it the way it has always been? (It has only been the previous two generations!)

How God Views the World

We see the world through the paradigms of our experiences and culture. The following maps are meant to show you a different paradigm of how God may see the world. Remember God sees everything and feels all that everyone is feeling.

Land Mass Map[1]

If you are like most people you see the world as the traditional land mass map below.

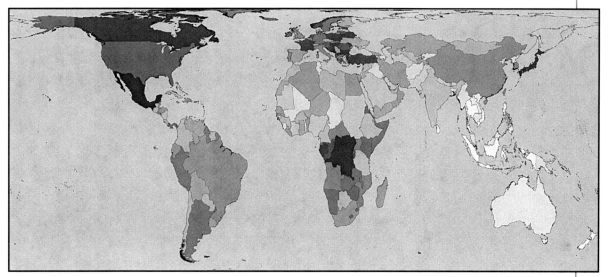

Population Density Map[1]

The following population density map takes the traditional land mass map and reapportions the size of each country to its population in comparison to the rest of the world.

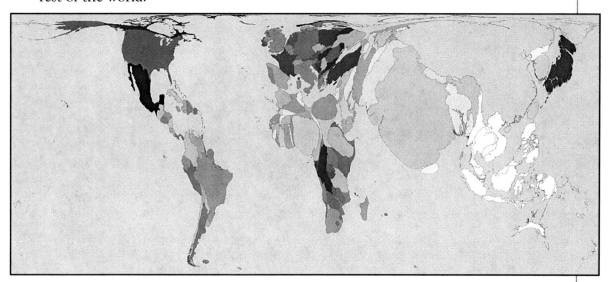

Infant Mortality Density Map[1]

This next map shows the ratio of infant mortality between countries—7.2 million infants and 3.2 million children between the age of 1 and 4 die each year.

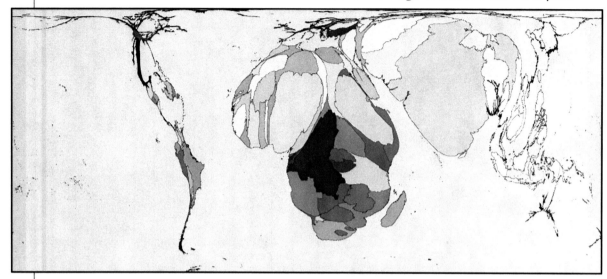

Poverty Density Map[1]

The following map is a population density map of people around the world living in poverty. 17% of the world's population lives on less than $1 per day and 43% on less than $2 per day.

Money Density Map[1]

This final map is a money density map of the countries around the world.

In 1989 the USA, Europe, and Japan had 74% of the world's money. But the map below shows the money density today with the emergence of China and India's economies. Don't let the map deceive you. China and India still have the largest number of people living on less than $2 per day. But the richest 5% of the people living in China, Europe, India, Japan, and the USA currently have close to 90% of the world's money.

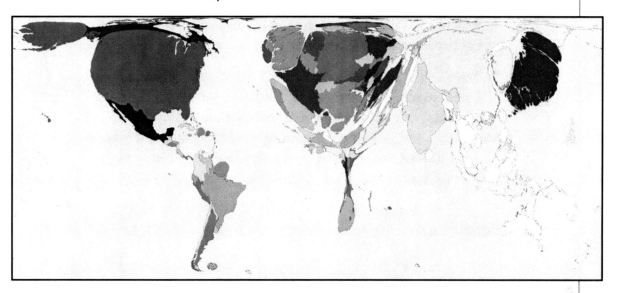

God's Judgment

"When the Son of Man comes in his glory, and all the angels with him, he will sit on his throne in heavenly glory. All the nations will be gathered before him, and he will separate the people one from another as a shepherd separates the sheep from the goats. He will put the sheep on his right and the goats on his left.

"Then the King will say to those on his right, 'Come, you who are blessed by my father; take your inheritance, the kingdom prepared for you since the creation of the world. For I was hungry and you gave me something to eat, I was thirsty and

you gave me something to drink, I was a stranger and you invited me in, I needed clothes and you clothed me, I was sick and you looked after me, I was in prison and you visited me.'

"Then the righteous will answer him, 'Lord, when did we see you hungry and feed you, or thirsty and give you something to drink? When did we see you a stranger and invite you in, or needing clothes and clothe you? When did we see you sick or in prison and go visit you?'

"The King will reply, 'I tell you the truth, whatever you did for one of the least of these brothers of mine, you did for me'

"Then he will say to those on his left, 'Depart from me you who are cursed, into the eternal fire prepared for the devil and his angels. For I was hungry and you gave me nothing to eat, I was thirsty and you gave me nothing to drink, I was a stranger and you did not invite me in, I was sick and in prison, and you did not look after me.'

"They will also answer, 'Lord, when did we see you hungry or thirsty or a stranger or needing clothes or sick or in prison, and did not help you?'

"He will reply, 'I tell you the truth, whatever you did not do for one of the least of these, you did not do for me.'

"Then they will go away to eternal punishment, but the righteous to eternal life." (Matthew 25:31-46)

Question 2:

Having seen the maps and read (Matthew 25: 31-46) where would you rate yourself on a scale of 0 to 10 with 0 being totally selfish and 10 being totally giving?

0   1   2   3   4   5   6   7   8   9   10

Why did you rate yourself the way you did?

_____

_____

_____

_____

Exercise:

When you get together with your group look on the label on the back of the shirt, blouse, or dress of the person next to you. Where was the article of clothing made?

How many countries are represented in your study group by the articles of clothing people are wearing?

Question 3:

Our "dinosaur thinking" causes us to want to use our blessings to collect things for ourselves. But much of the world doesn't have the financial blessings and freedom we have. Unless your shirt was made in the USA, why do you think God has given us greater financial blessings and freedom than the person who made your shirt?

_____

_____

_____

_____

Today, most of our churches say they don't have enough money to give to missions and local ministries. The lack of funding is not the problem. It is only a symptom of the real problem which is the "It's mine dinosaur thinking" that has infiltrated us, our churches, and the world. This keeps many of us from allowing Jesus Christ to be our true Lord and guide.

> *"Religion that God our Father accepts as pure and faultless is this: to look after the orphans and widows in their distress and to keep oneself from being polluted by the world." (James 1:27)*

Question 4:

Are you living a lifestyle that glorifies God with your blessing? How much more could God be glorified by you living a simpler lifestyle?

_____

_____

_____

_____

_____

_____

Reflections

Those who cling to worthless idols forfeit the grace that could be theirs. But I, with a song of thanksgiving, will sacrifice to you. What I have vowed I will make good. Salvation comes from the Lord. (Jonah 2:8-9)

And He died for all, that those who live should no longer live for themselves but for Him who died for them and was raised again. (2 Corinthians 5:15)

But store up for yourselves treasures in heaven, where moth and rust do not destroy, and where thieves do not break in and steal. (Matthew 6:20)

"He is no fool who gives up what he cannot keep to gain what he cannot lose." *Jim Eliot*

"So many suffer so much while so few sacrifice so little." *Bob Pierce*

"Possessions are not given that we may rely on them and glory in them but that we may use and enjoy them and share them with others…" *Martin Luther*

"Most people buy things they don't need with money they don't have to impress people they don't like." *Anonymous*

"We can choose to live more simply that others may simply live. There is enough to go around, but sharing our abundance with others will call us to cut back somewhere, to limit ourselves voluntarily, to live a lifestyle that reflects our knowledge of the condition of people in our world." *Paul Borthwick*

"The Bible seems adamant to warn us, to advise us and tell us not to accumulate, to collect and store up more and more things, but to give more and be deprived if Love called for it." *John Piper*

"What would happen to this world if more evangelical Christians were to realize that God blessed them with more money in order to make them a blessing, not to pamper them." *Ralph Winter*

"We make a living by what we get, but we make a life by what we give." *Winston Churchill*

Chapter Four
IMPATIENCE
(I Want It Now!)—Part One

4

Most People Are More Easily Influenced by the Instant Reward

Behavioral psychologists identify man's tendency to be more easily influenced by small, but immediate and definite rewards than he is by large, but distant and uncertain rewards. In other words, most people are more easily influenced by the instant reward, or good taste of a candy bar, than by the long-range reward of having a fit and trim body in six months if they were to stop eating junk food and start exercising.

"I want it now!" tendencies are impulsive. They are short-term actions with high emotional involvement, similar to how children act. Retailers understand and use this impulsiveness. Have you ever noticed the enticing goods that stores display by their checkout counters?

Have you ever seen a child throw a tantrum in a store to get what he wants? Kids are smart. They quickly discover where they can ambush their parents. Behavior they would never get away with at home is effective in the store because parents are afraid of what others may think.

Shopping with Beth

Years ago I enjoyed shopping with Bethany, our youngest child. Within a minute of entering a store, she would spot something she wanted. "Can I have this, Daddy?"

"You can have one thing. If that is what you really want, you may have it."

Soon she would see something else. "Can I have this, Daddy? Please, may I have this?"

"You can if you really want it. But if you do, you will have to put the other back."

"Please, Daddy, can't I have both?"

"I said you can have one thing. Now if you act up, you can't have anything. If you are good, you can have the one thing you want most, and you will have to put the other back."

"Okay." She would huff and return one of the items. But, in another minute she would see something else she just had to have. She would ask again, and I would explain again. By about the tenth time she would say, "Daddy, I want to put this back and go back to the animal crackers. Animal crackers are what I really want."

Another time after she had started school, Bethany asked, "Can I have this, Daddy?"

I answered, "No, I'm short of money."

She looked at me strangely. That wasn't part of our routine. "Please, may I have this?" she asked.

I picked up the item, showed her the price tag, and asked, "How much does this cost?"

Bethany studied it, and I showed her the 59-cent price tag. I told her if she could help me save 59 cents, she could have it. We started comparing the prices of different brand names of items on my shopping list. Soon we had saved enough.

What I was teaching my daughter was, Lord willing, we may obtain what is of value if we spend our money wisely, save, and avoid buying on impulse.

"I want it now!" is the predominant tenet of "dinosaur thinking" because too many people don't understand the delayed gratification of planning, working, and saving for the future. For instance, it takes a lot of discipline to save enough money to make a down payment on a house. In the USA, many chase a dream of winning the lottery. I know people living from paycheck to paycheck who spend $20 to $40 a week on lottery tickets. The chances of accumulating enough money in five or six years to make a down payment on a house by investing $20 to $40 weekly are over a million times greater than winning the money in the lottery.

Dinosaur thinkers do what is fun and easy. Colorful things that move and make noise always get their attention. That is why dinosaur thinkers love to watch television. It's easy on our brains. We don't have to think or imagine because the television lays everything out for us.

The entire dinosaur's brain is the part of our human brain called the brain stem or medulla. It is the medulla that controls our involuntary body functions like breathing, heartbeat, reflexes, and fight, flight, or freeze reactions for physical protection. It is from the "fight, flight or freeze" responses that "dinosaur thinking" is generated in man. God gave the dinosaur and mankind these reactions for protection from physical danger. The human "dinosaur thinking" happens when man uses the system God gave us for physical protection against perceived psychological threats.[1] We will discuss this in more depth in chapter nine.

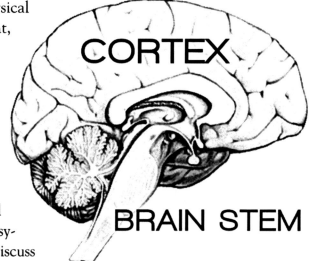

But the human brain also has a cortex, or higher brain, that was meant to help us overcome our lower "dinosaur thinking" tendencies. It is through the cortex that we dream, think, and imagine. But like a muscle, this part of our brain needs to be exercised to remain strong.

If you break an arm and have it set in a cast, its muscles weaken due to inactivity. When the bone is healed and the cast removed, you will strengthen it again through exercise. Likewise, if you don't use your brain, your ability to think and reason is diminished. An athlete's muscles must be in superb condition. She trains so that when she needs the extra strength, she can perform. In the same way, the more you exercise your brain, the more thinking and reasoning ability you'll have.

Did you know that ten minutes of reading stimulates your brain as much as four hours of watching television?[2]

All too often, children from industrialized nations come home from school and turn on the television, video game, or computer. They fully intend to do their homework. But, they want to see what is on next, or if they can win one more game. Before they know it, it's time to go to bed, and their homework is not done.

Scripture says, *there is a time for everything and a season for every activity under heaven. (Ecclesiastes 3:1)* The dinosaur wants what it wants, and it wants it now. Some "dinosaur thinking" Christians pray for God to help them win the lottery or for other shortcuts to acquire their wants.

> *"You want something, but don't get it. You kill and covet, but you cannot have what you want. You quarrel and fight. You do not have, because you do not ask God. When you ask, you don't receive, because you ask with wrong motives. That you may spend what you get on your pleasures." (James 4:2-3)*

Many Christians are frustrated because God doesn't answer their prayers in the way they think is best or in their time frame. God hears their prayers, but He is more concerned with their maturing than He is with their comfort and pleasure.

Question 1: (for discussion)
Does God answer all prayers?

The author thinks God answers all prayers. Three of His many answers are:

1. Yes
2. I will give it to you later after you have matured more in your faith.
3. No! You cannot have it because you ask with wrong motives, that you may spend it on your pleasures. (Remember Matthew 6:33)

Faulty Instant Evangelism

"I want it now!" thinking can also be seen in some evangelists. Several years ago, I had the privilege of delivering the funeral service for my great aunt, Aunt Flo. I had called on her regularly for three years prior to her death, and she loved to tell stories of how Jesus was her strength. During the service I shared her testimony and her prayer that all of her children and grandchildren would accept Jesus Christ as their Lord and Savior before they died.

A zealous Christian relative, who didn't know of Aunt Flo's conversion, challenged me after the service. He was surprised to hear she was a Christian. He told me he had thought about visiting her several times after he heard she was terminally ill. One day as he drove by her house on the way to a job he thought he should stop, but didn't have time. He felt guilty so he turned around about a mile past her home. As he entered her home he said, "Aunt Flo, I don't have a lot of time so I'll get right to the point. Have you accepted Jesus Christ as your Savior?"

Aunt Flo said, "If the only reason you stopped is to preach at me, you can just leave!"

"I'm really surprised to hear she was a Christian after she threw me out when I tried to witness to her," said my zealous relative.

I said, "Did it ever occur to you that your witness might be more effective if you would start off by saying hello and take some time to visit first?"

Don't Eat the Cow

The Heifer project is a good illustration of teaching overcoming "I want it now." I met Kwacha Chrsiza, Country Director of Heifer International—Zambia, when I visited his country in 2005. He told me that in the early days of the Heifer project, people would, more often than not, butcher and eat a cow when it was given to them. So they developed a program where a person would have to learn all about cows before she would be given one. She would also have to learn about the finances of how to care for a cow and how to manage the profits from the sale of its milk. She would have to work as an intern with a person who already was managing a small two or three cow dairy farm. Then once she was given a heifer, a young bred cow, she did not fully own it until after it gave birth to a calf, and she raised that calf until it was a bred heifer ready to be given away to another person who had gone through the training. Once she gave away her cow's first heifer, the cow she was given was hers. But if she butchered the cow before that, she would have to pay for it.

Kwacha Chrsiza said, "If you just give a person a cow, he will eat the cow. Heifer International will only provide a heifer to people who have completed their education and training. One heifer, when managed properly, can provide for all the needs of an African family and put their children through school. That heifer can multiply and become a blessing to an entire community."

I visited a small dairy farm of a lady who had been given a cow ten years earlier. From that one cow, she was milking 11 cows and provided work for 41 people.

Waiting on God

Many nations who have recently gained their independence have an "I want it now!" mentality. They immediately want wealth and power. That was not the goal of the founders of the USA back in its beginning in 1776. After God had delivered America from the tyranny of an oppressive foreign government, the American forefathers sought to establish a new country and government with Biblical principles to be one nation under God with liberty and justice for all. It was never their intent to become the world's most powerful or richest country. But it was their intent to give its people the freedom to put their Christian principles into practice as they worked and developed their family farms and businesses. The majority of Americans were dedicated Christians who trusted God through famines, floods, wars, political turmoil, natural disasters, and economic collapse during the first 175 years of its history before God blessed the nation as a super power.

Today, many Christian scholars say America has become a post Christian nation because too many Christians have lost their zeal to put God first. Their "dinosaur thinking" of "I want it now!" has led many Americans into debt and bankruptcy. Today, the majority of Americans who call themselves Christian are more concerned about self-indulgence on Sunday morning than worshipping God.

> *"Now if you obey me fully and keep my covenant, then out of all nations, you will be my treasured possession. Although the whole world is mine, you will be for me a kingdom of priests and a holy nation." (Exodus 19:5-6)*

There are no guarantees in life. People who trust in the Lord, set goals, make plans, follow through, and work hard are not always successful by worldly standards. But, if you have no goals or plans, and always do what is fun and easy, you won't accomplish much.

> *"Go to the ant, you sluggard; consider its ways and be wise! It has no commander, no overseer or ruler, yet it stores its provisions in summer and gathers its food at harvest. How long will you lie there you sluggard? When will you get up from your sleep? A little sleep and a little slumber, a little folding of the hands to rest—and poverty will come on you like a bandit and scarcity like an armed man." (Proverbs 6:6-11)*

The Law of the Farm

If you lived on a farm and you wanted to harvest your crops in the fall, you would have to plow and ready the field for planting in the spring. Then you would have to plant your seed. During the summer you would have to cultivate and hoe. Lord willing, you could harvest your crop in season. This illustrates "the law of the farm" which is to reap a harvest you must plan ahead, and do what needs doing when it needs to be done.[3]

Now suppose you shirked your responsibilities all spring and summer watching television, golfing, and playing computer games. As harvest season comes, you can't plow, plant, cultivate, and harvest all in the same week. It is too late. Everything worth anything in life is under "the law of the farm."

People who spend most of their time doing what is fun and easy, and then cram at the last minute to do just enough to get by, usually are not successful.

We see this with students with poor study habits. They are ultimately exposed to another universal truth: God can't help you remember what you never learned. Their "dinosaur thinking" makes them blame their failure on bad luck.

There is no such thing as luck. The truth is we can all experience what dinosaur thinkers call luck when we understand luck is when preparation meets opportunity.

Question 2:

What examples of "I want it now!" thinking have you seen?

_____

_____

_____

_____

_____

_____

_____

_____

_____

_____

One example is a person not having enough money to pay his rent at the beginning of the month because during the previous month he bought things he didn't need.

Question 3:

In industrialized nations like the USA, too many Christians seem to have the goal to go from birth to death with the maximum amount of comfort and the least amount of pain. Is this also true in developing nations? Is it Biblical?

_____

_____

_____

_____

_____

A better question might be, "Is this true of you?"

_____

_____

Would you remain faithful and obedient to God if your relationship with Him caused you to be hated so much by your brothers that they would throw you into a well until they could sell you as a slave? Then after years of loyalty and success for your master you were thrown into jail because of lies; then after spending years in jail helping fellow prisoners and guards, you were forgotten by an ex-prisoner who promised to help you when he got out? Many Christians believe that if you believe, God should never allow you to go through pain and suffering. That wasn't the case with Joseph whom God used to save Israel.

> *Then Joseph said to his brothers, "Come close to me." When they had done so, he said, "I am your brother Joseph, the one you sold into Egypt! And now, do not be distressed and do not*

be angry with yourselves for selling me here, because it was to save lives that God sent me ahead of you." (Genesis 45:4-5)

But Joseph said to them, "Don't be afraid. Am I in the place of God? You intended to harm me, but God intended it for good to accomplish what is now being done, the saving of many lives." (Genesis 50:19-20)

Joseph was used greatly by God, but he never preached. God blessed him with an understanding of management and business operations. God used him to bless his people because Joseph was faithful and didn't give into "dinosaur thinking" tendencies.

Question 4:

What area of understanding is God giving you?

_____

_____

_____

_____

_____

_____

_____

_____

_____

Question 5: (for discussion)

"And surely I will be with you always, to the very end of the age." (Matthew 28:20b) Does this mean Christians should always expect health and wealth? Give the reason for your answer?

> **"I have told you these things, so that in me you may have peace. In this world you will have trouble. But take heart! I have overcome the world." (John 16:33)**

Question 6:

How is impatient "dinosaur thinking" hindering you from being able to bless God's people?

The ladies in one church we visited in India saved a handful of rice each day from their cooking. On the first Sunday of each month they brought their saved rice to the church. The church distributed the rice to the needy and sold some rice to raise money to help the church meet needs.

Question 7:

How is God glorified by you blessing others?

_____

_____

_____

_____

Question 8:

We told several stories in this chapter. Which one connected best with you to help you understand the importance of over-coming "I want it now dinosaur thinking?"

_____

_____

_____

_____

Reflections

"Failure for the believer is always temporary. God loves you and me so much that he will allow almost any failure if the end result is that we become more like Jesus." *George Verwer*

However, I consider my life worth nothing to me, if only I may finish the race and complete the task the Lord has given me. (Acts 20:24)

"Behold, I am coming soon! My reward is with me, and I will give to everyone according to what he has done." (Revelation 22:12)

Now listen, you who say, "Tomorrow we will go to this or that city, spend a year there, carry on business and make money." Why you do not know what will happen tomorrow. What is your life? You are a mist that appears for a little while and then vanishes. Instead you ought to say, "If the Lord wills, we will live and do this or that." As it is, you boast and brag. All such boasting is evil. Anyone then who knows the good he ought to do and doesn't do it sins." (James 4:13-17)

The difference between man and the dinosaur is man can be responsible. Man can dream and set goals. Man can make plans to accomplish his goals, and, Lord willing, it will happen. But, the fact a man can do something doesn't mean he will. The first step for him to succeed is to overcome his "dinosaur thinking."

Chapter Five

IMPATIENCE

(I Want It Now!)–Part Two

5

Using "I Want It Now!" for Training in Positive Behavior

This chapter uses stories to illustrate how "I want it now dinosaur thinking" tendencies of responding to immediate and consistent rewards while avoiding instant punishments can be used to help overcome "dinosaur thinking." Negative behavior can be changed into positive behavior for both children and adults. This is frequently seen in the cartoon of a donkey that has a carrot dangling in front of him to lead him in the direction the owner wants him to go, and a boot attached to a contraption that will kick him in the rear every time he does something he is not supposed to do.

Behavior psychology has discovered that the size of a reward or punishment does not motivate nearly as much as a consistent and immediate delivery of a reward or punishment.

For instance, would your driving change if your car had a device on the dashboard that would loudly buzz when you went one mile per hour over the speed limit?

Would you be more motivated to obey the speed limit if every time the device buzzed, you were fined one dollar and your total fines would automatically be deducted from your next pay check?

Basic Behavior Modification

When I was a counselor-house parent at George Junior Republic I created a curfew policy. I had a cuckoo clock that made its sounds on the hour, half hour, and quarter hour. The boys had to be in the house with the door shut before the clock made its sound. On the first night I implemented the curfew, a couple of the boys were standing on the porch talking and entered the house when they heard the clock. I didn't yell. I asked them how their night went as I marked on the board that their curfew for the next night out would be ½ hour earlier.

The late boys yelled, "We were in on time. What are you doing taking a half hour off our curfew?"

I calmly said, "You were outside the door when the clock sounded. You then opened the door and came in. You were at least three seconds late."

They said, "What type of an idiot are you? You're burning us for being three seconds late!"

I said, "It would be best for you to think of me as being an immediate and consistent idiot when it comes to enforcing curfew violations. It doesn't take a lot of brains to observe whether or not you are in the house with the door shut before the cuckoo coos."

The next Friday night all the boys were in before the cuckoo cooed except one who was hanging on the open door talking to a friend on the street. When the clock made its sound, he jumped in the house and closed the door.

I asked him if he had a good night as I marked a half hour off his Saturday night's curfew.

"I was in on time," he said.

I said, "The rule is you have to be in the house with the door shut before the clock makes its sound. You were hanging on the open door when the clock sounded and then came in and shut it. You were at least one second late."

"What the _ _ _ _ is the matter with you burning me for one second!"

I said, "Now you have lost another half hour for swearing. Now think before you say anything else. You have only lost one half hour for being late and another half hour for swearing. Is it really worth risking being grounded and losing all of your privileges?"

His higher brain was in a battle with his dinosaur brain. The outcome was he decided being grounded was worth the satisfaction he received in telling me off and having the last word.

We had no curfew violations over the next few weeks. Then one of the boys came in a half hour late. He was afraid I would be angry and apologized profusely. He said he was late because he helped a friend change a flat tire.

I said, "Sacrificing a couple of hours off your next night's curfew to help a friend is commendable. I'm proud of you."

He asked, "Do I still lose the two hours?"

I said, "Yes. If you knew you would lose two hours off your next night's curfew if the same thing happened again, I hope you would still help. Sometimes something may come up that may be worth losing some time. That's your choice."

From that time on I never had a curfew problem. That doesn't mean they were always in on time. But when they were a little late, they would ask me what time it was and go over to the board and change their curfew time for the next night they were allowed out.

You may think I was overly strict for busting them for being one second late. But this prevented the hassle from the boys' testing the limits. Once their "dinosaur thinking" understood that they would receive an immediate punishment when they violated the curfew, even though it was small, the program ran smoothly. The clock was a blessing because being in the house with the door shut before the cuckoo cooed eliminated all subjectivity as to being in on time.

Hank, the Relief Man

The Pub, the nickname for George Junior Republic, had difficulty back in the 70's finding good regular relief help. I had worked four or five months without a day off. Finally we hired Hank as my relief. With him as regular relief, I could work ten days on and have four days off.

I carefully reviewed the house rules with Hank. I emphasized the importance of consistency in applying the house rules, and that it was not good for the boys if the relief man is buddy buddy with them and doesn't follow the house rules. The boys needed consistency. I carefully went over my curfew policy and told him that like a substitute teacher in a class for the first time, the boys most likely were going to test him on the curfew.

He found it hard to believe that I wanted the boys disciplined if they were one second late. I told him the discipline was only a half hour. Knowing that each and every time they violated the curfew would result in a predictable action, even though it was small, would be like swatting them lightly with a fly swatter. The problem with many parents is they only give warnings for small violations. They continue to give unheeded warnings as the violations escalate until they get angry and ground their kids for a month. Grounding a youth for a month after several warnings is like trying to correct him with a blast from an elephant gun. Consistently administering small rewards or punishment, like a light tap with a fly swatter, is easier and more effective than punishing them with a severe and long discipline after repeated and unheeded warnings. Hank agreed to enforce all of the house rules and to be totally consistent with what I had in place.

Hank and all the boys were happy when I returned from my four days off. I asked Hank if any of the boys tested him. He said they were all good, and he enjoyed the time with them. I was surprised that none of them tested him with the curfew.

I worked the next ten days, and Hank came to relieve me for my four days off. This time when I returned, the boys were happy, but Hank wasn't as happy. He assured me that everything went fine. Again, I expressed my surprise that none of the boys tested him.

But the next time when I returned, the boys were happy, but Hank was visibly upset. I talked with him in my office. He insisted that everything was fine. I asked, "Were there any curfew violations?"

He said, "No."

I asked, "Were all of the house rules followed by the boys?"

He said, "Yes."

I asked, "Were you totally consistent with the written house rules?"

He said, "Dave, I have everything under control."

I asked, "You have everything under control?"

Hank said, "Yes."

I said, "I have a feeling that there is something you are not telling me."

I worked my next ten days, and this time when I returned from my time off everyone was upset. Hank told me that he had grounded two of the boys, Ed and Zeke, for two months and two other boys, Bud and Brad, for a month.

I asked, "What in the world happened that you want to punish me for the next two months?"

Hank said, "Ed and Zeke were a few minutes late in getting back to the house on the first Saturday night I worked. But, I had a meeting with them and told them that I would not bust them for being a few minutes late, and I wouldn't tell you if they promised not to be late again."

I said, "Okay, that was the first weekend. What happened the second?"

Hank said, "Ed and Zeke came in about an hour late. I'm pretty sure they had been drinking. Bud and Brad came in about fifteen minutes late."

I said, "You didn't mark that on the board or tell me about it. What did you do?

Hank said, "I had a house meeting. I told them that I didn't want to bust them, but some of them were starting to take advantage of me. I didn't want to get them in trouble. They promised not to do it again."

I said, "Okay, that was the second weekend. Tell me what they did on the third."

Hank said, "Ed and Zeke didn't get in until 2:45 in the morning. They were drunk. Bud and Brad came in an hour late."

I asked, "What about Chas and Herb?"

Hank said, "They were in on time."

I said, "Good for them. Now tell me about the meeting you had that third weekend."

Hank said, "I got really mad at them for walking all over me. I told them that I wouldn't say anything to you if they would promise not to be late or get drunk on me again."

I said, "And they promised that they wouldn't?"

Hank said, "Yes. But I warned them if they did it again, I would ground them for at least a month."

I said, "Okay, that brings us to this weekend."

Hank said, "Ed and Zeke didn't get home until after daylight, 7:30 in the morning. They had hangovers. Bud and Brad came in at 2:00. I grounded Ed and Zeke for two months and Bud and Brad for a month. I'm teaching them a lesson that they can't walk all over me.

I said, "What would have happened if, on the first Saturday you worked here, you would have taken a half hour off Ed and Zeke's next Saturday night's curfew?"

Hank said, "Dave, I could never bust a kid for only being five minutes late."

I said, "Hank, you're fired!"

The Amazing Chas

I sat with Chas in my office looking at his report card the morning of his high school graduation. His family was coming. We were having a party for him at the halfway house after commencement. He was officially being released and returning home with his parents at the end of the day. It was a day to honor Chas' achievements, but I was stunned with his report card. I had seen Chas slowly change from a boy, who didn't feel he was worth anything, into a young man with confidence. Seeing his report card for the entire year objectively showed the change in him.

I said, "Chas, it has been an honor for me to be your houseparent this past year. As a counselor for this institution, I know I'm good. But when I see how you have changed over the past year as this report card objectively shows, I know I'm not that good. Please tell me how you did this."

Chas' Report Card

SUBJECT	1ST 6 WKS	2ND 6 WKS	3RD 6 WKS	4TH 6 WKS	5TH 6 WKS	6TH 6 WKS
Phys. Ed	F	C	C	B	A	A
Sr. English	F	D	C	B	A	A
Jr. History	F	D	C	A	A	A
Sr. History	F	D	B	B	A	A
Sr. Science	F	D	A	A	A	A
Sr. Math	F	D	C	A	A	A

Chas said, "Dave, I accepted Jesus Christ as my Lord and Savior because of your prayers. I remember the first day I came here. You prayed as we were all sitting at the dinner table. I had never heard anyone pray like you. It was so different from the grace we said at the main campus of the Pub which was usually, 'Good food, good meat, yea God, let's eat.' When you prayed, it was as if Jesus was sitting at the table. You prayed specifically for each one of us. You thanked God for bringing me to your house. You prayed for me to adjust to the new rules, and that I would learn to see the potential of what I could do in my life. Jesus was real to you. I actually looked around the room as you prayed to see if He was there."

I said, "Wow. You just told me that my prayers led you to Jesus Christ, and I hadn't realized it. When did you accept Jesus?"

Chas said, "It was right after the first report cards came out. I had met Laura at school, and I wanted to go out with her. I pleaded with you to bend the rules and let me stay out past 9:30 on Friday night. But you said I had to be passing all my subjects to earn that privilege. It was frustrating because I had never done well in school. Having Fs on my report card was just who I was. That night I lay crying in bed. For the first time I prayed, 'Jesus if you are real help me talk to you the way Dave does.' A peace came over me, and I started talking to Him. I told Jesus that I was tired of being a failure and asked Him to help me. I asked for forgiveness because I had never tried to do well. I cried myself to sleep. I started to read the Bible that was in my room. I prayed myself to sleep each night, and in the morning I prayed to do well at school.

I was excited when the second report card came out. It was the first time since the eighth grade that I had passed all my subjects. I was excited that I could be with Laura on both Friday and Saturday nights. But I was angry at you for not allowing me to stay out past 10:00. You said for me to be allowed out until midnight, I would have to be working at my full potential in school. I thought just passing everything was my full potential. But you insisted that I could do better."

"I remember that conversation, but I never dreamed that you could make all A's," I said.

"I didn't either," said Chas. "I started to study a little bit at home and prayed that I could make all C's. Then on the third report card, I got an A and a B and the rest were C's. You allowed me to stay out until 11:00 on Friday nights."

"But as I prayed that night, I realized that I wasn't trying my hardest. I wondered just how good my grades could be if I really tried. Also, I was a little afraid you might move me back a step if my grades went down. So I decided I would give my absolute best in school. It felt good getting all A's and B's on the fourth report card. I thanked God that He showed me if I put my mind to do something, I could do it. And then it happened. I got all A's. I did better than I ever imagined. My teachers say I should go to college. What do you think?"

"Why not?" I said.

Question 1:

How does a person who comes into the Kingdom and is grateful to God for sending Jesus to save him from Hell, see his relationship to God?

_____

_____

_____

_____

_____

_____

_____

If you knew that you were going to spend eternity in Hell, but now are saved through Jesus Christ and now know you are going to Heaven, would you be grateful to your Lord and Savior?

Would you want to know more about this Jesus who saved you?

Would you want to read your Bible to learn more so you can become a better follower of Jesus?

Would you want to tell others that He, who saved you, could also save them?

Would you want to become more involved in your church and in serving Him?

Would you want to spend more time in prayer?

Do you think you might change as you develop a mindset of being grateful to God and wanting to glorify Him?

Might you become more patient, more kind, more gentle, and develop more self-control?

Of course your answers should be yes to all of the above.

As this happens in your life, would you become more valuable to your employer? If you are a salesperson or business owner and start caring more for your customers, do you think you might get more customers and have more sales?

Of course you would.

The primary reward of repenting of your sins and accepting Jesus as Lord and Savior is you will be with Jesus in Heaven for eternity. Being a better person here on earth is a side benefit that comes naturally to you when you remember the main thing is to give all glory to God because of who He is and what He has done on the cross.

"I want it now dinosaur thinking" seekers are not motivated by the big reward of Heaven or by the big punishment of Hell in what they hope will be the distant future. Without repentance, they come to Christ for an immediate reward of improving their life or getting help out of a mess.

In the late 1800's, more than 80% of Christian converts remained long-term in the church. Back then, people came to Christ as repentant sinners. They understood when they died they would either be going to Heaven or Hell. Knowing they were sinners and could not get to Heaven on their own, they confessed their sins, and were grateful to God for sending Jesus to die for their sins.

Today less than 20% of the American converts remain in the church the rest of their lives.[1]

Question 2: (for discussion)
Why do you think more than four out of five new converts to Christianity in America quit going to church in less than a year?

Patient Evangelism Destroyed
by I Want It Now!

Jim contacted me several years after he left our specialized foster care program. He had been in our program longer than anyone else because his parents deserted him, moving out of state shortly after he was placed with us. I picked him up from jail one morning. He had served a one month sentence for public drunkenness and disorderly conduct. He had lost his job, had a restraining order to stay away from his girlfriend, and had no money or place to live. Through the grace of God, Jim turned to me for help. I was able to share the love of Jesus Christ with him. I witnessed to Jim with my time and money. I invited him into my home, hired him to help me paint my house, and took him to places where he could meet and hear from other witnesses.

That evening I took him to a regional men's Christian meeting. The speaker gave an invitation. Jim wasn't ready to accept Christ as Lord. He came with me because he didn't have any place else to go and because I cared for and helped him. However, he distrusted preachers. His father was a preacher who had physically and verbally abused him. Jim had Attention Deficit Disorder, and his dad thought he could preach and beat it out of him.

Jim said, "How will I know when I'm ready to invite Jesus into my life?"

I said, "I think of it as ABC. First you must A, **accept**, that you are a sinner unable to change on your own. (**Romans 3:23**) says, *"For all have sinned and fall short of the glory of God."* and (**Romans 6:23**) says, *"for the wages of sin is death, but the gift of God is eternal life in Christ Jesus our Lord."* Then you must B, **believe**, that Jesus is who He says He is, the Son of God who came into the world to die for our sins. (**John 3:16** says), *"For God so loved the world that He gave His only Son, that whoever believes in him shall not perish but have eternal life."* Then C, **confess**, (**Romans 10:9-10**) says, *"That if you confess with your mouth, 'Jesus is Lord' and believe in your heart that God raised Him from the dead, you will be saved. For it is with your heart that you believe and are justified and it is with your mouth that you confess and are saved."* Then I said, "Jim, do you accept that you are a sinner?"

Jim said, "No! I've done some dumb things, but I'm not a murderer or bad criminal or anything like that."

I said, "I'm glad you are honest in telling me you feel that way. Scripture says, *"For Christ died for sins once and for all, the righteous for the unrighteous, to bring you to God." (1 Peter 3:18.)* Romans 5:8 says *"But God demonstrates His own love for us in this: While we were still sinners, Christ died for us."* It would be hypocritical of you to ask Jesus into your life if He says He died for your sins, and you don't think you are a sinner.

Jim said, "Yeah."

The rumor was out in the meeting that Jim had just gotten out of jail, and the evening's speaker wanted to lead him to the Lord. After repeated invitations where Jim did not go forward, the speaker's "I want it now dinosaur thinking" could not wait any longer, and he came back to where Jim and I were sitting.

The speaker said to Jim, "Are you tired of all the troubles you are having in your life?"

Jim shook his head, "Yes."

The speaker said, "Would you like Jesus to deliver you from your troubles? Would you like Jesus to restore your broken relationships? Would you want Jesus to find you a job?"

Jim nodded, "Yes"

The speaker said, "Stand up!"

Jim stood and the speaker put his hand on his forehead and said, "In the name of Jesus be delivered from all of your troubles."

Jim fell down, and everyone in the room cheered but me. The speaker was happy. He got a big notch on his belt for winning to Christ a poor soul who had just gotten out of jail. But Jim accepted Jesus without having repented.

Jim went to church with my family. I gave him a Bible, but he didn't read it. After a month he said, "I don't want to go to church any more. I tried Christianity, and it didn't work. My girlfriend still won't talk to me, and none of the things that man promised happened."

Question 3:

Can a person who hasn't repented become a real believer in Jesus Christ? Why or why not?

_____

_____

_____

_____

_____

It took me a long time to truly ask Jesus into my life. I have never liked to be pushed into anything; therefore, I don't try to push others to believe. I have often messed things up when I've pushed for something that felt right to me, but I hadn't sought the Lord's guidance or prayed about it. My guiding scriptures for witnessing are:

> **"But in your heart set apart Christ as Lord. Always be prepared to give an answer to everyone who asks you to give the reason for the hope that you have. But do it with gentleness and respect." (1 Peter 3:15-16a)** and **"Let us not become weary of doing good, for at the proper time we will reap a harvest if we do not give up." (Galatians 6:9)**

When I pray, "God's kingdom come, His will be done," I'm praying that my witness in word and deed will bring people closer to Jesus and not drive them further away. I know that God is in control, and sometimes people do accept Christ with a true conversion the first time they hear. But I can become frustrated with evangelists who convert people that they have never seen before and whom they most likely will never see again. Too many times these converts are not repentant and have no one to disciple them. They too often slip out the back door of the church as fast as they came in the front. Once they have slipped away, they are harder to reach again.

Question 4:

Can you find any place in the Bible that says we are to make converts?

_____

_____

_____

For several years now, I've offered to give $100 to anyone who can show me in the Bible where Jesus tells us we should go and make converts. No one has ever found it.

> In the Great Commission, Jesus says, **"All authority in heaven and earth has been given to me. Therefore go and make disciples of all nations, baptizing them in the name of the Father and of the Son and of the Holy Spirit, and teaching them to obey everything I have commanded you. And surely I will be with you always, to the very end of the age."** (Matthew 28:18b-20)

Jesus commands us to make disciples. If a person becomes a convert while being discipled, he will most likely develop into a mature believer and remain long-term in the church.

Question 5:

Can you find any place in the Bible that says we are to go and plant churches?

_____

_____

_____

If our emphasis is properly placed on discipleship, God will use us, and we will have converts accepting Him and becoming disciples, and we will have churches planted.

Jesus told His disciples that they would become fishers of men. In the American sport fishing paradigm, we think of fishing as one person with one pole and one line, catching one fish at a time. But in Jesus' day, fisherman fished in small groups with nets. Only 10 to 20 percent of their time was actually on the water fishing. Most of their time was making, mending, and caring for the nets. Because they took time with their nets, (making relationships in the process) they often caught hundreds of fish at a time.

Jesus commissioned us to make disciples, and making disciples takes time. We need to spend time with the people we are discipling. When we disciple and witness this way to the people God leads us to, they become converts who will become good disciples and witnesses that will be part of an effective long-term ministry within a church.

Reflections

"For I know the plans I have for you," declares the Lord, "plans to prosper you and not to harm you, plans to give you hope and a future." *(Jeremiah 29:11)*

"Now if we are children, then we are heirs, heirs of God and co-heirs with Christ, if indeed we share in His sufferings in order that we may also share in His glory." (Romans 8:17)

"...but one thing I do: Forgetting what is behind and straining toward what is ahead, I press on toward the goal to win the prize for which God has called me heavenward in Christ Jesus." (Philippians 3:13-14)

"What we are is God's gift to us. What we become is our gift to God." *Louis Nizer*

"The purpose of life is a life of purpose." *Robert Byrne*

"Man's mind, stretched to a new idea, never goes back to its original dimensions." *Oliver Wendell Holmes*

Chapter Six
BLAMING & COMPLAINING
(Hissing)

6

*"A Man's Own Folly Ruins
His Life, Yet His Heart
Rages Against the Lord."*
(Proverbs 19:3)

A dinosaur thinker never sees himself as the source of his trouble. When things go wrong, his "dinosaur hissing" leads him to find someone to blame and then complain. Dinosaur thinkers often form support groups where everyone complains and sustains each other's distorted view of reality.

The "dinosaur hisser" blames, complains, grumbles, and murmurs. He never takes responsibility. Whenever anything goes wrong, he always protects his tail. We see this in people who say, "It's not my fault!"

Delta

Delta was one of my best employees. However, she aggravated me when anything went wrong by saying, "It's not my fault!" In most situations there was no way it could be, but she had to say it.

One day I was particularly frustrated when one of our suppliers sent us the wrong item for the second time. She immediately said, "It's not my fault!" Hearing that was like being hit in the mouth.

I yelled, "Don't you care that this order is messed up? Don't you care that I'm frustrated? Don't you care that our customer will be upset and disappointed? I know it's not your fault!" She was about to cry. Then I said, "Whenever anything goes wrong, why can't you just say, 'I'm sorry.' Does saying I'm sorry mean you're at fault?"

"No."

"The next time you get the urge to say, "It's not my fault!" can you just say I'm sorry instead?"

She was silent, then smiled and said, "I'm sorry, Dave." I never heard her say, "It's not my fault!" again. This is an example of overcoming the "dinosaur hissing" tendency to protect one's tail.

Imitation Mayonnaise Destroys Witness!

This story of "dinosaur hissing" illustrates how uncontrolled disappointment may hurt your witness. Back when I was a Young Life leader I took my young friend, Bob, out for lunch. He was excited because he was going to give his testimony at our next meeting. It was the first time he had ever been asked to speak. Bob ordered a cheeseburger with lettuce, tomato, onion, and real mayonnaise. He made a point that it must be real mayonnaise and not an imitation salad dressing.

Bob practiced his testimony as we waited for our food. After it arrived, we prayed. Bob prayed God would make him a good witness and show him the areas he needed to work on. After he said Amen, he took a bite of his cheeseburger. His "dinosaur hissing" took control of him. He stood up saying, "Damn it, I told her I wanted real mayonnaise!"

He yelled, "Miss, Miss, this is not what I ordered!"

The young waitress returned. "What's wrong?"

"I told you I wanted real mayonnaise and not salad dressing!" Bob said. "This is salad dressing! When I asked you to make sure it was real mayonnaise you should have asked the cook! If you don't have real mayonnaise, I would have ordered mustard and onions."

I said, "Bob, calm down! It is only a sandwich!"

"When I was a waiter, I took all kinds of crap if I screwed up. When I eat in a restaurant I expect my waitress to listen to me."

The waitress started to cry.

I told her, "I'm sorry for his behavior." I asked, "Do you know there is a difference between mayonnaise and salad dressing?"

She said, "No."

"Many people don't know there is a difference, and most people who know don't care," I said. "But once in a while you will come across a real jerk that will make an issue of it."

By this time the manager was with us, and everyone in the restaurant knew there was a difference between mayonnaise and salad dressing. The restaurant did not have real mayonnaise. The waitress had asked the cook, but he didn't know that the salad dressing he used wasn't real mayonnaise. After apologies from everyone, Bob finally got a cheeseburger with mustard and onions, but he was too upset to eat it. "Dinosaur hissing" can really upset a person's digestive system.

I said, "Bob, how old do you think the waitress is?"

"Sixteen, maybe seventeen," he said.

"Is she still in high school?"

"Most likely," he said.

"We always get a few new kids to come to the meetings. If she comes, how do you think she will feel when she sees you? When you stand up to speak, will she hear anything you say?"

Poor Jake

Jake was an aggressive evangelist. I met him the first time I went to a Christian businessman's meeting in his home city. Having never seen me before, he grabbed me by the arm and said, "DO YOU KNOW JESUS? HAVE YOU MADE HIM YOUR SAVIOR? IS HE YOUR LORD? ARE YOU READY TO BE SAVED?" The next thing I knew, he had me in a bear hug jumping up and down, yelling, "YOU'RE GOING TO BE SAVED! YOU'RE GOING TO BE SAVED!" I wanted to run. I tried to think of an escape route. But I broke out into a belly laugh. How could I sneak out when I was the guest preacher?

My mother knew Jake, and a few months later I heard her ask his employer if Jake worked for him.

"Oh yes. He works for me."

"Has he won you to Jesus?" my mother asked.

"He sure has tried," the employer said. "I told him if I wanted to hear about his Jesus, I would go to church. But while he is working for me, I'm paying him to work, and I don't want to hear it and don't want him bothering my other employees."

"You don't let Jake witness?" my mother asked.

"Not from 7 to 3. But he'll get in a 'You need Jesus!' when he walks out the door."

"Well, have you accepted Jesus?" my mother asked.

"No," the employer said as he smiled.

"Why not?"

"When Jake is not telling someone they need Jesus, he complains about how tough everything is for him and his family," the employer said. "No! I don't want anything to do with Jake's religion. How could I expect his God to take care of me when he doesn't take care of Jake all that well?"

The Stolen Bicycle

This following story illustrates how "dinosaur hissing" can dull a person's memory. Upon leaving church in a third world country, a man couldn't find his bicycle. He immediately reported to the pastor that someone from the church had stolen it. He yelled at the pastor that Christians shouldn't steal. The pastor agreed and asked the man to preach that evening. The pastor said that theft was too common a practice in that area, and the church needed to hear that Christians should not steal.

The man decided to preach on the Ten Commandments. His plan was to briefly cover each of God's laws and to really give the congregation a piece of his mind when he got to the eighth commandment, *"Thou shalt not steal."* His hope was to shame the person who had stolen his bicycle into returning it. His sermon went well until he got to the seventh commandment, *"Thou shalt not commit adultery."* At this point, he remembered where he had left his bicycle.

Six Million Dollar Mistake

This next story illustrates a leader who has overcome "dinosaur blaming and complaining." Several years ago, an IBM salesman made a mistake in writing up an order for a large company. Correcting the error cost IBM $6,000,000. The CEO of IBM had the young salesman flown in to meet with him. If the salesman had been a dog, he would have had his tail between his legs. When he met the CEO he said, "I guess you are going to fire me."

The CEO said, "Fire you! Are you crazy, we just spent $6,000,000 on your education."

What would have happened if the CEO had fired him? Would other young sales people take risks? How many times have you done something perfectly right the first time you tried to do it? What was it like the first time you ever tried to ride a bicycle? Did you fall a few times? As a child, your desire to learn to ride your bicycle was so strong that you were willing to take the risk of falling.

There is no such thing as "trial and immediate success." We call it "trial and error." When we want to master something, we go through "trial and error," "trial and error," "trial and error," before we see a "trial and success." If you are afraid to make a mistake, you will never try anything or accomplish much. Yet all too often our "dinosaur I want it now thinking," which we learned about in the last two lessons, drives us to expect immediate results and our "dinosaur hissing" tends to make us want to blame and complain when we don't get what we want. Many churches scrap ideas after only one attempt at implementation. A year or so later, another person will suggest the idea again, and it will be voted down because "We tried that once." They are quick to judge the idea and the person who tried it as failures.

Dinosaur thinkers can be very critical and judgmental. Jesus said: *"Judge not, that you be not judged" (Matthew 7:1)* Jesus' instructions in regard to judging others are very simple. DON'T! Yet, many Christians are piercingly critical. Criticism is one of the daily activities of dinosaur thinkers. But in the spiritual realm, nothing is accomplished by it. The effect of criticism is the dividing of the strengths of the one being criticized. The Holy Spirit is the only one in the proper position to show you areas in your life that need to be improved, and He alone is able to show what is wrong without hurting and wounding. It is impossible to enter into fellowship with God when you are in a critical mood. The criticism that comes with "dinosaur hissing" serves to make you harsh, vindictive, and cruel, and leaves you with the soothing and flattering idea that you are somehow superior to others. Jesus says that as His disciple, you should cultivate a temperament that is never critical. Overcoming your "dinosaur thinking" tendencies will not happen quickly, but must be developed over a span of time. You must constantly be aware of the thoughts which cause you to think of yourself as a superior person.

Question 1:

What examples of "dinosaur hissing" have you observed?

You see this type of thinking every time you hear someone blame or complain.

Question 2:

What can you do to help yourself stop blaming, complaining, grumbling or murmuring?

_____

_____

_____

_____

_____

_____

_____

Meditate on These Verses

Do everything without complaining or arguing, so that you may become blameless and pure, children of God without fault in a crooked and depraved generation, in which you shine like stars in the universe. (Philippians 1:14 & 15)

I consider that our present sufferings are not worth comparing with the glory that will be revealed in us. (Romans 1:20)

If anyone considers himself religious and yet does not keep a tight rein on his tongue, he deceives himself and his religion is worthless. (James 1:26)

Therefore, rid yourselves of all malice and all deceit, hypocrisy, envy, and slander of every kind. Like newborn babies crave pure spiritual milk, so that by it you may grow up in your salvation, now that you have tasted that the Lord is good. (Peter 2:1-3)

And do not grumble, as some of them did-and were killed by the destroying angel. (1Corinthians 10:10)

Don't grumble against each other, brothers, or you will be judged. The judge is standing at the door. (James 5:9)

The People Rebel

That night all the people of the community raised their voices and wept aloud. All the Israelites grumbled against Moses and Aaron, and the whole assembly said to them, "If only we had died in Egypt! Or in this desert! Why is the Lord bringing us to this land only to let us fall by the sword? Our wives and children will be taken as plunder. Wouldn't it be better for us to go back to Egypt? And they said to each other, "We should choose a leader and go back to Egypt."

Then Moses and Aaron fell face down in front of the whole Israelite assembly gathered there. Joshua, son of Nun, and Caleb, son of Jephunneh, who were among those who had explored the land, tore their clothes and said to the entire Israelite assembly, "The land we passed through and explored is exceedingly good. If the Lord is pleased with us, he will lead us into that land flowing with milk and honey, and will give it to us. Only do not rebel against the Lord. And do not be afraid of the people of the land, because we will swallow them up. Their protection is gone, but the Lord is with us. Do not be afraid of them." (Numbers 14:1-9)

The Israelite grumbling and murmuring was the equivalent to "dinosaur hissing." The people wanted everything given to them instantly without having to show their faith in God. They quickly forgot what God had done for them when they saw the risk of going into the land of milk and honey. Seeing they could not do it on their own, they grumbled and murmured instead of trusting and believing God's promise. God threatened to destroy them, but Moses interceded for them in prayer.

Question 3:

Can we be a good witness for Jesus Christ if we blame, complain, grumble, and murmur? Give reasons for your answer.

Question 4:

A.   Were the Israelites forgiven for their complaining and grumbling against Moses, Aaron, and God?

B. What were their consequences?

_____

_____

_____

_____

The Lord replied, "I have forgiven them, as you asked. Nevertheless, as surely as I live and as surely as the glory of the Lord fills the earth, not one of the men who saw my glory and miraculous signs I performed in Egypt and in the desert but who disobeyed me and tested me ten times- not one of them will ever see the land I promised on oath to their forefathers. No one who has treated me with contempt will ever see it. (Numbers 14:20-23)

Question 5:

Even though God can forgive our sins of blaming, complaining, grumbling, and murmuring, what could be the consequences of our sinning this way?

_____

_____

_____

_____

Remember Bob, the young man who wanted real mayonnaise, and Jake, the aggressive evangelist. Their complaining hurt their witness. There could be hundreds of consequences. The point is there are consequences.

Question 6:

How do you feel when you are around a person who always blames and complains?

_____

_____

_____

_____

Question 7:

As a Christian witness and disciple of Jesus Christ, what changes do you need to make in your life to become a better witness?

_____

_____

_____

_____

_____

_____

Exercise:

1. When you find yourself blaming, complaining, grumbling, or murmuring ask yourself:

   ■ What will I gain by punishing someone who has made a mistake or inconvenienced me?

   _____

   _____

   _____

   ■ What can I do to help fix the problem?

   _____

   _____

   _____

2. When you are with others who are blaming, complaining, grumbling, or murmuring:

   ■ Ignore them.

   ■ Answer their bad with good.

   ■ Ask, "What are you going to do about it?"

   ■ If that person is complaining about you, ask, "Can you please tell me what I can do to satisfy you?"

Almost all Americans were outraged when the Twin Towers in New York City were destroyed on 9/11/2001 by Islamic terrorists. I'm sure God was saddened by the deaths of the 2,800 people killed that day, and He will judge the people responsible.

The following charts may illustrate how God's heart for the surviving loved ones from that terrorist act could compare to His heart for other surviving loved ones of people around the world that day.

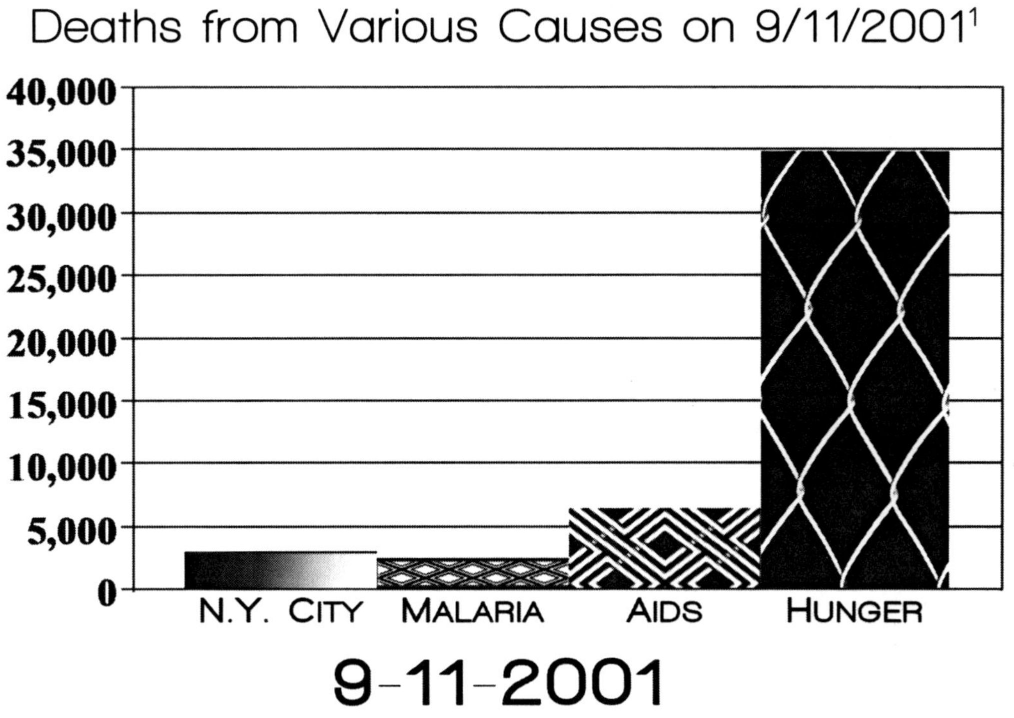

Deaths from Various Causes on 9/11/2001[1]
40,000
35,000
30,000
25,000
20,000
15,000
10,000
5,000
0
N.Y. CITY
MALARIA
AIDS
HUNGER
9-11-2001

Question 8:

Do you think on 9/11/2001 that God was hurt just as badly by the cries and pains of the families of the 2,400 people who died of malaria, the 6,200 people who died of AIDS, and the 35,000 people who died of hunger as He was from the 2,800 families who lost loved ones in the Twin Towers?

Question 9:

God feels the pain and suffering of each person who dies every day and the hurt of their survivors.

A. Why do you think most Americans are oblivious to the number of people around the world who die each day from malaria, AIDS, and hunger?

_____

_____

_____

B. How many people are dying each day from malaria, AIDS, and hunger without ever hearing of Jesus Christ?

_____

Question 10:

Our "dinosaur hissing" is quick to make us blame, complain, and grumble when we suffer the least disappointment or delay while at the same time so many of us have been insensitive to the pain and suffering of others around the world. If this is true of you, does it bother you? Why or why not?

_____

_____

_____

_____

_____

When Jesus was asked for the greatest commandment in the Law, He replied:

"Love the Lord your God with all your heart, and with all your soul, and with all your mind. This is the first and greatest commandment. And the second is like it: "love your neighbor as yourself." All of the Law and Prophets hang on these two commandments." (Matthew 22:37-40)

Question 11:

Does God consider the people who die around the world each day from malaria, AIDS, and hunger to be neighbors to us Christians? Explain your answer.

Now you may be thinking God is in control, and He can't be expecting you to try to do something to help the poor, sick, and hungry around the world dying without Christ. But no Christian has a special exemption from being part of the Great Commission where Jesus tells us to *"go and make disciples of all nations, baptizing them in the name of the Father and of the Son and of the Holy Spirit, and teaching them to obey everything I have commanded you." (Matthew 28:19-20a)* Also, none of us are given an exemption from the commandment to love our neighbors.

Think of God's desire for your work in the Great Commission and the Great Commandment as if you owned a business. What type of people would you want working for you? Wouldn't you want hard working dependable employees who cared about the success and image of your business? Wouldn't you want confident employees who have overcome their "dinosaur thinking" who work together to accomplish their assigned tasks? Wouldn't you want people who jump in to do what they can to help when difficulties arise? Of course the answer is yes to these.

Now suppose your business makes a large profit because your employees who have understood your vision and objectives make excellent products and deliver them with timely and effective service to your customers. Wouldn't you want to reward your people? [2] Wouldn't this be like the master rewarding those who had been trustworthy as found in the parable of the Ten Minas? (A mina = 3 months' wages.)

The Parable of the Ten Minas

While they were listening to this, he went on to tell them a parable, because he was near Jerusalem and the people thought the kingdom of God was going to appear at once. "A man of noble birth went to a distant country to have himself appointed king and then to return. So he called ten of his servants and gave them ten minas, 'Put this money to work,' he said, 'until I come back.'

"But his subjects hated him and sent a delegation after him to say, 'We don't want this man to be our king.'

"He was made king, however, and returned home. Then he sent for the servants to whom he had given the money, in order to find out what they had gained with it.

"The first one came and said, 'Sir, your mina has earned ten more.'

"Well done, my good servant!' his master replied. 'Because you have been trustworthy in a very small matter, take charge of ten cities.'

The second came and said, 'Sir, your mina has earned five more.'

"His master answered, 'You take charge of five cities.'

"Then another servant came and said, 'Sir, here is your mina; I have kept it laid away in a piece of cloth. I was afraid of you, because you are a hard man. You take out what you did not put in and reap what you did not sow.'

"His master replied, 'I will judge you by your own words, you wicked servant! You knew, did you, that I am a hard man, taking out what I did not put in, and reaping what I did not sow? Why then didn't you put my money on deposit, so that when I came back, I could have collected it with interest?'

"Then he said to those standing by, 'Take his mina away from him and give it to the one who has ten minas.'

"'Sir,' they said, 'he already has ten!'

"He replied, 'I tell you that to everyone who has, more will be given, but as for the one who has nothing, even what he has will be taken away. But those enemies of mine who did not want me to be king over them-bring them here and kill them in front of me.'" Luke 19:11-27

Question 12:

What story or Bible verse used in this chapter has made you think the most? Why?

_____

_____

_____

_____

_____

_____

_____

_____

_____

Reflections

"Whatever you do, work at it with all of your heart, as working for the Lord, not for men, since you know that you will receive an inheritance from the Lord as a reward. It is the Lord Christ you are serving." (Colossians 3:23-24)

"People seem to not realize that their opinion of the world is also a confession of character." *Ralph Waldo Emerson*

"God, grant me the serenity to accept people that drive me crazy; the courage to get up and going; and the wisdom to know you love the bananas out of me even when I screw things up?" *Hugh Myrrh*

Chapter Seven
TWISTING THE TRUTH
(Get the Mate)

7

"Dinosaur Thinking" Wants
Someone to Take Care
of Us and/or Someone
We Can Control

"**G**et the mate dinosaur thinking" deals with more than courtship rituals. It can also be seen in business, politics, churches, and social organizations. It occurs when a person or organization sees an attractive potential partner who they feel could help them or who would make them feel good if they helped. In other words, our "dinosaur thinking" wants someone to take care of us and/or someone we can control. When our "dinosaur thinking" perceives a potential partner it leads us to want to embellish our stories so we can appear bigger, better, and more attractive than we really are, just like a turkey that puffs up its chest and spreads its tail feathers.

God Told Me You Will Give Me Money

I first became aware of "dinosaur get the mate thinking" back when I was in business. A Christian couple, who had heard me speak at a church program, asked to meet with me. They said God had given them an idea for a business, and they were praying for God to lead them to Christian venture capitalists to invest in the start-up cost. I interrupted them as they were saying that God led them to me.

I asked, "Have you been to a bank to see how much money you could borrow from the equity in your home?"

The wife responded, "We would never put our home at risk to invest in a business!"

I said, "Borrowing on the equity in our home is what my wife and I did to start our business, and you are fooling yourselves if you think God led you to me to invest in your idea when you don't have enough faith in it to risk anything of your own."

I then told them what I think of people that say, "God told me!" as a means to manipulate Christians.

God Told Me You Will Hire Me

A pastor friend of mine tells of a similar situation. He was on a committee to hire a Christian camp director. One of the candidates on the first day of interviewing told the committee that God told him he was going be the new camp director. At the end of the meeting, some of the committee members said there was no need to meet again to interview the remaining candidates because God had told the one applicant he was getting the job.

My friend said that God hadn't told him that person would be the new director and insisted they interview the other candidates before making the final selection. The committee met the following week and quickly interviewed the remaining candidates.

After the interviews, the vote was to hire the man who said it was God's will for him to be the new camp director. When they contacted him, he informed the committee that he had accepted another position.

Question 1:

Do you think God told that person he was going to be the camp director? Why or why not?

_____

_____

_____

_____

_____

God can speak to us, and the Holy Spirit definitely leads when we seek to be in His will. But some people develop a habit of saying "God told me" as a means to convince people to give to them or let them do what they want. This "Get the Mate" thinking wants to manipulate you into agreeing with it. It is like he is trying to place a devil on your shoulder that says if you disagree with him, you are disagreeing with God. It works closely with "I want it now" because it wants you to make a quick decision. Remember that the devil is a great deceiver. He doesn't have to put evil ideas in your head that may create harm or lead people away from God if your "dinosaur thinking" will do it for him. The devil only has to deceive you into thinking the idea is God talking to you or the Holy Spirit's leading.

To overcome this, you must first know the Bible by developing a daily reading time. You then need to pray the Lord gives you discernment in knowing the difference between what God says and what the devil would like you to think God said. Remember in the Lord's Prayer, **"Give us this day our daily bread."** Use this to pray for what you need to know each day and that God will lead you to the resources you need.

> *Now the serpent was more crafty than any of the wild animals the Lord God had made. He said to the woman, "Did God really say, 'You must not eat from any tree in the garden'?"*

The woman said to the serpent, "We may eat fruit from the trees in the garden, but God did say, 'You must not eat fruit from the tree that is in the middle of the garden, and you must not touch it, or you will die'."

"You will not surely die," the serpent said to the woman "For God knows that when you eat of it your eyes will be opened, and you will be like God, knowing good and evil."

When the woman saw that the fruit of the tree was good for food and pleasing to the eye, and also desirable for gaining wisdom, she took some and ate it. She also gave some to her husband, who was with her, and he ate it. (Genesis 3:1-6)

Help That Destroyed an Economy

Several years ago, a pastor visited a mission during a severe famine. He had compassion for all of the starving people and as soon as he returned home, he started to raise funds to send them food. A year later as the local farmers were harvesting their crops, his large shipment of food arrived. The drought that had caused the famine the year before had ended with abundant rains during that current growing season. The farmers had one of the best crops ever, but the value of the crop was 90% less because the shipload of free food arrived just as the harvest was beginning. Farmers threw up their hands and said, "We can't afford to plant next year if we can only get 10% on the value of the crops we produce." [1]

The above story is another example of "get the mate dinosaur thinking." It was so easy for a big-hearted Christian believer to catch a plane and go to a remote area of the world. He saw what he saw and acted on his feelings to help without knowing their local culture, economic system, or anything about farming. Raising money and sending food made him feel good. Because he felt the idea was of the Holy Spirit, he didn't see a need to consult with career missionaries and local leaders living in the area who would have advised him differently, nor did he contact a disaster relief organization. Ultimately we need to prayerfully develop local leadership in any ministry. If we don't respect our third world Christian brothers as potential leaders that God can also use, we run the risk of teaching them to become dependent on us.

The great commission also tells us to teach them (local leaders we should be discipling) *"to obey everything Jesus has commanded us."(Matthew 28:20a)*

"Religion that God our father accepts as pure and faultless is this: to look after the orphans and widows in their distress and keep oneself from being polluted by the world." (James 1:27)

The devil works hard to deceive Christians into thinking that God is speaking to them, when in actuality, it is their "dinosaur thinking." It must give the devil great joy when our impatient "I want it now dinosaur thinking" works with our "get the mate dinosaur thinking" to make decisions that feel good and excite us. As we saw in the preceding story, great damage can be caused where projects are hastily organized without much prayer or thinking through the consequences. Short-term missions should always come under the authority of the career missionaries, national ministry, or mission leadership. It would have been far better for our big-hearted pastor to coordinate his efforts with a disaster relief organization that needs funds to react immediately when and where help is needed.

Help That Destroyed Years of Work

A Wycliffe missionary told me of how a short-term American mission team destroyed years of missionary work in a restricted country. A church sent a short-term team to visit the area where the missionaries had lived and worked. No one on the team asked the missionaries how they could help or what they needed to do to prepare for the trip. The team came with their American agenda of which visiting the missionaries was part. This church had done several evangelical outreaches in America, and felt the same kind of outreach would work in this restricted country.

The natives were polite to the short-term strangers who spoke to them through interpreters. But after the strangers returned home, (I'm sure they had great reports of all they had done.) the tribal leaders went to the missionaries. The leaders told the missionaries that they liked them, but they never understood why they lived among them or what they were doing. The tribal leaders then told the missionaries they were no longer welcome because the strangers told the tribe of a new religion that was not part of their tribal culture and explained to them that the missionaries were working so that one day their new religion would destroy all that the tribe had always believed.

Making a Con Man

The following is an example of "dinosaur get the mate thinking" that can hurt individuals by giving to them. It also illustrates how an individual can use "dinosaur get the mate thinking" to manipulate others to give him what he wants.

Brad was one of the youth under my care back in the mid-1970's when I was a counselor/parent. Brad's coming under my care was his fifteenth placement since he was abandoned at a hospital door when he was an infant. He was then placed into a foster home of a loving couple who cared for him as their own child until welfare removed him.

Brad loved his first foster parents and still referred to them as mom and dad. He visited them from time to time, and they kept in contact with Brad by letters and visited him shortly after he was placed in the halfway house. Brad's removal from them was very sad. His foster mother told me they had him from birth for seven years and a pair of twins for five years. They took on four other children for a short time when their county didn't have any place else to put them. With seven foster children, they came to the attention of state authorities who inspected them and found them in violation of several regulations. To come into compliance with the rules it was determined that they could only keep two children. Giving up Brad was the hardest thing his foster mother had ever done. She loved Brad and thought of him and the twins as her own.

Brad was in his second foster home for less than a week. He couldn't understand why he was put there and wanted to go back to his mommy. He was more than the new foster parents could handle, and child welfare put him into a third foster home. From there he went in and out of several group homes before he came to George Junior Republic when he was fifteen. This was the first placement since his removal from his first foster parents in which Brad adjusted well. After a year in the institution, I was asked to take him into my halfway house. The goal of this placement was to help him adjust to a home-like environment for the next two years. It was hoped that he would graduate from public high school and be released as an adult, able to live normally in society.

Before Brad had come down to the halfway house, he met Amanda, a twenty year old college Junior, who was doing volunteer work. She continued seeing him. Brad thought it was great because she drove a sharp new car, an Oldsmobile Cutlass Supreme. I allowed him to go with her to McDonalds and to a movie. I never thought about a romance between them. Before long she was wearing a ring Brad had given her, and he was wearing her college ring on a chain around his neck.

I had a talk with her. She told me she loved Brad. In that conversation I discovered she lived sixty miles away, and Brad was calling her every day. I told her that Brad never talked about her. He only talked about how much he loved her car.

After Amanda left, I talked with Brad. He told me he loved her because she cared more and did more for him than any other woman he had known. I asked him if it occurred to him that she might be nuts. He assured me that their love was real, and that the age differences meant nothing to them. Brad was dumbfounded when I asked how he was going to pay for his long distance phone bill. (It was a lot more expensive to talk long distance in the pre-cell phone days.)

Brad said, "Don't worry man, I'll pay for it."

"With what?" I said, "You have been fired from the three summer jobs I got you! And your allowance between now and Christmas most likely won't be enough to pay it."

"You're crazy. It can't be that much," he said.

That night after dinner, Beatrice, another girl who was eighteen and out of high school, stopped to visit Brad. I surprised them as I walked through the living room. They were lying on the couch making out.

After Beatrice left, I said, "Brad, you told me earlier today that you love Amanda."

"I do," he said.

"What's going on with you and Beatrice?"

"Nothing, she is just a friend," he said.

"Does she know that?"

"She understands me," he said.

"Does she know about Amanda?"

"Yeah, she knows."

"Does Amanda know about her?"

"Amanda doesn't need to know. What she doesn't know won't hurt her."

When the phone bill arrived, Brad was surprised that his calls cost more than $200. He didn't like it that I barred him from using the phone until he had his phone bill paid in full.

A few weeks later, the institution arranged for Brad to go to a one week summer church camp. He was full of joy upon returning home because he had been given $100 to help pay his phone bill.

"Brad, you expect me to believe that people just gave you $100?" I asked

He said, "People just like to give me money. It happens all the time."

I called the camp director to verify Brad's story. The director told me how Brad had accepted Jesus Christ, how he gave his testimony, and how he was trusting Jesus to pay his phone bill. The director organized a love offering and said Brad was surprised when they gave it to him the last day of camp.

The halfway house was closed the last two weeks of August for vacation. All the boys went home with the exception of Brad who had no home to go to. I took him with me for the week of my vacation where I went with a local church to help build a youth camp in Kentucky.

On the third night in his small group session, Brad accepted Jesus again and told everyone his life history of being abandoned and unwanted. He told about his long distance phone bill, and how he was going to trust in Jesus to be able to pay it. I couldn't believe how people started giving him money. I tried to stop them, and no one would believe me that Brad had claimed to have accepted Jesus several times before and that Brad had manipulated them. No one believed me when I said giving him money was leading him into becoming a con man. They were upset with me for trying to deny them the good feelings they had of helping someone less fortunate.

During the large group meeting on the last night of camp, Brad went forward to tell how he had accepted Jesus earlier that week. It felt like the people were going to stone me when I refused to allow them to take up a love offering. Brad's "dinosaur get the mate thinking" led him to tell the good Christian people what they wanted to hear so he could make them want to give. Their "get the mate" dinosaur thinking led them to give because it felt good. They certainly did not think or pray about how best to help Brad before giving.

Question 2:

Did the people giving Brad money at the church camps help or hurt him? Explain your answer.

_____

_____

_____

_____

_____

_____

I lost track of Brad after he graduated from high school. About ten years later, I heard that he was doing time in a state prison because he had been caught in several con jobs.

I gave you a lot of background information on Brad's childhood to help you understand, to a small degree, why he developed into the person he was. Please don't get sidetracked thinking about everything that went wrong with the system. That is not the purpose of this story. However, if you are interested, I recommend an excellent resource to help you understand how to help in both domestic and foreign ministries: *WHEN HELPING HURTS, How to Alleviate Poverty Without Hurting the Poor and Yourself,* by Steve Corbett & Brian Fikkert, Moody, 2009

Deceiving Supporters

A mission-minded American pastor who worked exclusively with one developing world indigenous ministry asked me to visit his ministry when I traveled through the city where it was based. The American pastor had shown me brochures of the great work of the ministry and pictures of his last trip where he had spoken to its 200 pastors. So I visited the ministry accompanied by an indigenous missionary friend who had taken my training. We visited other indigenous ministries and missions. During one of these visits, I was asked, "Can

God bless a ministry that never actually tells an outright lie, but exaggerates the truth to make it look bigger, better, and more productive than it actually is?" Prayerfully researching to answer this question expanded my understanding of "dinosaur get the mate thinking."

I discovered that the American pastor's ministry was actually working with less than 20 pastors, not 200. The ministry's executive director was on the board of directors of other small ministries. Their executive directors were on his board of directors. Each of the ministries was receiving donations from churches from industrialized nations. These donations bought and maintained nice offices and cars for the ministries. Many of the executive directors hired relatives to staff their office, drive their ministry's car for their personal use, and live in extravagant homes.

When a pastor and/or mission team of any of the supporting churches came to visit any of the small ministries, the director of that ministry would invite the directors of the other ministries to bring all of their people to a large meeting to hear the visitors speak. At the visiting speaker's expense, the local ministers were often paid a per diem to come, and meals were always provided.

The visiting pastors were told that the poverty in the country was so great that many of the attendees could not attend without the per diem and meals. (Depending on where the training occurred and who was invited, this may or may not be so.) However, paying people to come guaranteed a large audience, and in many cases, the cost of feeding everyone was much less than what was charged.

Often, the visiting speaker thought all who attended the meetings were with the ministry his church supported. Though the directors of the indigenous ministries knew what was happening, most of their people had no idea that any deception was occurring and praised God for the opportunity to come and learn to be better servants of the Lord Jesus Christ.

Some of these indigenous ministries publish nice newsletters and magazines to keep their supporters informed and to solicit funds. Every positive thing the ministry can find happening in its area is reported. Projects done by other ministries and missions are written about, often without any acknowledgement or credit given to them. Everything reported is basically true. However, missing from the newsletter is the fact that the ministry publishing it may not have done any of the work, nor contributed financially to it. Though the ministry does not say it did the work, the reader would assume it did.

The above is certainly not true of most pastors, directors, ministries, and missions. However, it happens often enough in both the developing and industrialized nations that we need to be aware of our "get the mate dinosaur thinking" that tends to make us want to embellish the truth.

Question 3:

"Can God bless a ministry that never actually tells an outright lie, but exaggerates the truth to make it look bigger, better, and more productive than it actually is? Explain your answer.

We would like the answer to be no. But many indigenous people have been blessed by coming to special events organized by ministries' leaders and paid for by the visiting short term missionaries. Some indigenous ministry leaders live well from what they make from their connections with American churches and missions. They feel this is acceptable because they are doing God's work, just as expatriate missionaries had done before them, and they should be able to live like the American missionaries did. However, we will all face the Judgment, and I wouldn't want to be one of the ministry leaders who succumbed to his "get the mate dinosaur thinking" of keeping most of the money for himself that was given to help the needy.

Lying to God

Now a man named Ananias, together with his wife, Sapphira, also sold a piece of property. With his wife's full knowledge he kept back part of the money for himself, but brought the rest and put it at the apostles' feet.

Then Peter said, "Ananias, how is it that Satan has so filled your heart that you have lied to the Holy Spirit and have kept for yourself some of the money you received for your land? Didn't it belong to you before it was sold? And after it was sold, wasn't the money at your disposal? What made you think of doing such a thing? You have not lied to men but to God."

When Ananias heard this, he fell down and died. And a great fear seized all who heard what happened. Then the young men came forward, wrapped up his body, and carried him out and buried him.

About three hours later his wife came in, not knowing what had happened. Peter asked her, "Tell me, is this the price you and Ananias got for the land?"

"Yes," she said, "That is the price."

Peter said to her, "How could you agree to test the Spirit of the Lord? Look! The feet of the men who buried your husband are at the door, and they will carry you out also."

At that moment she fell down at his feet and died. Then the young men came in and, finding her dead, carried her out and buried her beside her husband. Great fear seized the whole church and all who heard about these events. (Acts 5:1-11)

Ananias and Sapphira's "get the mate dinosaur thinking" made them lie so they would look better than they actually were. They sold their property, gave part of the money to the Apostles, but said they gave it all.

Question 4:

Did God ask them to give all of their money?

Question 5:

How might the story be different if Ananias and Sapphira had been totally honest saying, "We praise God that we sold our property for a good price and want to give a percentage of it to the ministry"?

Ananias and Sapphira wanted the same attention Barnabus received from the people for giving all the money from the sale of a piece of his property, (Acts 4: 32-37) and at the same time they wanted to keep much of what was already theirs. What they lacked was integrity. God would have surely blessed them if their desire had been only to glorify Him. But their attempt to deceive the church cost them their lives.

A Church Lies On Its Recommendation

I knew of a church that discovered some mental and character issues with their new pastor a few months after he arrived. They thought they had done everything right in looking for their new minister. His resume was impressive, he conducted himself well during the interview, his first sermon was excellent, and he was highly recommended by his previous church.

A few months later, a member of the church visited some relatives from the town where the pastor had last ministered. His relatives couldn't believe his church had called their old pastor to be its new pastor. They told horror stories of the problems they had with him.

The church member said, "Why wasn't any of what you are telling me on your church's recommendation?"

His relative said, "To get rid of him, we offered him a six month severance pay and to give him a good recommendation if he would resign."

Question 6

A.   Have you ever embellished the truth to get a job?

B. Have you ever told a lie to try to make a problem go away?

_____

_____

_____

_____

If your answer was yes to either of these, you know first-hand how "get the mate dinosaur thinking" works.

Question 7:

What examples of "get the mate dinosaur thinking" have you observed?

_____

_____

_____

_____

_____

_____

An example that irritates me during election season is the negative campaign ads we see on TV that twist the truth about candidates. The "dinosaur thinking" is "I have a better chance to win if I make the other person look bad."

Question 8:

Have you observed it in yourself? How is the Lord leading you to overcome it?

_____

_____

_____

_____

_____

_____

   The purpose of this chapter is to help you understand "get the mate dinosaur thinking." It is not to turn you off to giving. So here are a few examples of missions and churches working together with no "get the mate dinosaur thinking."

Outreach Training in Baja Mexico

   Colleen and I have helped organize some American outreach teams to evangelize migrant Indian farm workers in Baja Mexico. The teams were led by Philip, an experienced Global Recordings Network missionary. He liked to take American teams to an area three consecutive years during harvest season. Prior to bringing the Americans down the first year, he went to the villages close to the migrant Indian farm camps to recruit local Mexican churches and missions to partner with the Americans. Philip told the churches how he planned to have an evangelical outreach to the Indians at the migrant farm camps with the combined Mexican and American team. Many of the locals had never been on a mission outreach to the Indians. While helping the Americans, the local Christians saw that the Americans, who for the most part were not fluent in Spanish, couldn't accomplish much without them.

The second year to the same area, more local Christians volunteered because of the stories they heard from those who had helped the first year. We got them more involved with the technical part of the mission by using the diagnostic and duplication machines provided by Global Recordings Network. Once languages and dialects of the Indians in the camps were identified, the duplication machines made cassettes or CDs of gospel messages in the Indian languages for them. (There are about 300 Indian languages and dialects spoken in Mexico.) As we left the second year, Philip encouraged the local Christians to do the work by themselves.

During the third year, we took a small inexperienced American team back to the area. The local Christians got more involved in all aspects of the outreach and concluded that they could indeed do the work by themselves. We provided the local Christians with the needed supplies and equipment to continue the outreach after we left. Philip didn't bring the Americans back the fourth year, but started new outreach training in another area instead.

Free Clinic in Ecuador

A pastor who heard me share about the work of Global Recordings Network asked me to meet with a lady in the local hospital who coordinated a Christian medical mission team to work in a free clinic in the mountains of Ecuador for a week each year. The pastor told me the team was frustrated with not being able to share the gospel. Their medical expertise was greatly used, and they helped hundreds of people. But the medical team communicated through interpreters, and they were so busy working 12 hour days in the clinic that they never had an opportunity to share Christ with anyone. They decided to buy and take one hundred Spanish Bibles to give away.

The coordinator was excited when she told me this year they would share Jesus Christ by giving away Bibles. Her facial expression changed when I asked how many people coming to a free clinic in the mountains of Ecuador would be able to read the Bibles. She exclaimed, "How else can we share Jesus with them?"

I showed her the cassette tapes we had with gospel messages. I showed her the hand cranked tape player to play the tapes if the listener didn't have electricity. I then showed the Good News story-telling picture flip chart with pictures that accompany the Good News recordings in Spanish, some Ecuadorian Indian languages, and more than 1,000 other languages. I arranged for her team to take some of these recordings and Good News flip charts.

Two high school girls, who were daughters of team members, went with them. One had taken Spanish 3, and the other had taken Spanish 4. The first day at the clinic they played the recordings and turned the pages to the picture book in the waiting room of the clinic. It was like a Vacation Bible School lesson that repeated every hour. Everyone who came to the clinic heard the Good News! The girls' level of fluency was good enough that by the end of the first day they didn't need to keep playing the recordings. They could tell the Bible stories using the flip charts. They shared Jesus with everyone and led several people to the Lord.

Whose mission was this? It was the hospital's medical outreach. I simply made the arrangements to supply the medical team with GRN's Good News flip-charts and recordings which gave them a simple and effective way to witness to the people who came to the clinic. But the mission's ministry and outreach was theirs. There was no "get the mate dinosaur thinking" to control anyone. When the medical team left, the girls gave the Good News recordings and flip charts to the clinic so other medical teams could use them.

Reflections

"Do your best to present yourself to God as one approved, a workman who does not need to be ashamed and who correctly handles the word of truth." (2 Timothy 2:15)

"The world and its desires pass away, but the man who does the will of God lives forever." (1 John 2:17)

"God's unity is certainly in the midst of diversity, but meanwhile we need a greater Biblical, compassionate strategy for releasing finance. At the same time, we need the highest level of reality and integrity in all our fund raising." *George Verwer*

"If we have a further end in view, we do not pay sufficient attention to the immediate present; if we realize that obedience is the end, then each moment as it comes is precious." *Oswald Chambers*

"Visionaries are never willing to shelve God's vision simply because the resources appear to be unavailable... One of the most remarkable truths about vision is that when the vision is implemented, the result is creating, rather than consuming resources." *George Barna*

Chapter Eight
JUDGING OTHERS
(If You are Not Like Me—You are Bad)

8

If You are Like Me—You are Good; If You are Not Like Me—You are Bad

The dinosaur thinker divides everything into two categories. You are either one of us or one of them. If you are one of us, you are part of the herd. In other words if you look like me, act like me, think like me, then you are good. But if you are not like me and act and think differently than I do, then you are one of them. A bad one of them who is bigger, faster, stronger, and picks on me is a predator; and a bad one of them who is smaller, slower, weaker and I can pick on is prey.

Question 1: (Think about this paragraph and then answer the question)
Life experience teaches us that there are two kinds of people. One believes in working hard and being dependable. They are responsible, warm, and caring. They take care of their families, give to their churches, and help those in need. The other kind

wants everything handed to them. They put themselves before everyone and everything. They are not dependable. They don't care about helping others. They only care about getting what they want and to have fun. (Which kind of person are you?)

_____

_____

_____

_____

_____

_____

If you are like most people, you see yourself as the first kind and a lot of other people as the second. This is how "dinosaur thinking" distorts reality. There is nothing in that paragraph but a two category system of good and evil.

IF YOU ARE LIKE ME—YOU ARE GOOD; IF YOU ARE NOT LIKE ME—YOU ARE BAD

The above categorization is easy to believe. But there is no actual information. There are no facts given. The descriptions are vague. However, all of the statements have strong moral connotations. This is the essence of "dinosaur thinking." Don't let your dinosaur brain present the world to you in terms of: right/wrong, good/evil, us/them, etc. To overcome your dinosaur brain, demand and use facts to make your decisions and form your opinions." [1]

They Ought to Wear Clothes

An example of "if you are not like me—you are bad dinosaur thinking" was at an evening church program when I was about ten. Two missionary ladies spoke, and they had what was, at that time, the newest in technology, a Super 8 mm movie. This movie had no sound and the projector made a tic, tic, tic sound when it played. WOW! They were showing a movie of the naked people they worked with in the South Pacific.

During the question and answer session, an elderly lady of the church asked, "Is the main reason you're a missionary to teach those people that they ought to wear clothes?"

The one missionary lady said, "No. The only reason we are missionaries is to win them to Jesus Christ. After you die and go to heaven, you are going to find a lot of naked people running around up there."

Do As I Say!

Another example of "if you are not like me—you are bad" that created strong dinosaur emotions of "domination and territorial dinosaur thinking" happened one summer when I was in college. I worked a week at a textile mill. I had a guaranteed wage, but could make more money if I did more work than the quota set for my job. After a few days, I figured out a way to do my job much more efficiently than I had been taught. When the shop steward saw my work card, he said, "There is no way that you could have done that much work."

I said, "Look, isn't the work done?"

He said, "How did you do that much work?"

I showed him. He then ripped up my work card and wrote me up a new one. He marked that I had done only one unit over the quota. Then he said, "Don't ever do what you showed me again. Do it the way I taught you."

"Why!" I said, "If the company pays us for the work we do, why can't I be paid more if I figure out a more productive way?"

"You do as I say," the steward said. "You are on a probationary period here, and if I don't recommend you after 90 days you'll be fired."

"In 90 days, I'll be back in college," I said.

"Let me make this very clear," he said. "If you go showing you can do that much work, management will change the quota on your job and will look into other jobs and change those quotas. We are not going to let a punk college kid make that happen. So if you do it again the least that will happen to you is you will have a leg broken and the worst is you may be dead."

I quit that day. Within five years the company closed that plant and started a new factory in the south.

Pancake Pig

Our "dinosaur if you are not like me—you are bad thinking" is quick to tell us the way others do things is bad if it is different from how we do them. It can be embarrassing as we instinctively try to teach this to our children. My mother said that one of her most embarrassing times was when she went to pick up my older brother, Charlie, from the home of a friend. He was eating pancakes with the family. Charlie asked Mom if it was okay if he had one more pancake before he left. She agreed, and Charlie took a pancake, put butter and jelly on it, folded it in half like a sandwich, and took a bite out of it.

This was different from how Mom taught him to put a pad of butter in the middle of the pancake, pour some syrup on it, cut it up into pieces, and eat it with a fork. Mom yelled, "Charles Emery Derby, you don't eat like a pig at home, and you should not eat like a pig at your friend's house!"

His friend's mother said, "But that is the way we always eat pancakes."

Cultural Differences on Lying

My first experience of "dinosaur if you are not like me—you are bad thinking" in missions was in 2001 when I was asked by an American college outreach ministry if I had the contacts to organize a mission project for Guatemalan mountain villages. I asked Jose, a missionary friend visiting from Honduras, to coordinate the project. He had arranged a team of 6 Mexican Gospel Recordings missionaries, 11 Guatemalan evangelists, and 2 Guatemalan Campus Crusade missionaries to work with our 12 American college students. I praise God that I was able to coordinate the American part of the team and to raise the funds needed, but I wasn't comfortable being the project leader in Guatemala because

I wasn't fluent in Spanish, and I had never been to the country before. Jose said he would arrange for Hector, his Mexican missionary friend, to lead the project.

My wife, Colleen, and I were not able to be with the team the first week because we were teaching at a mission conference. We met with Jose when he came to escort the Americans to Guatemala to make sure everyone got connected. I had heard that Hector could only be there to lead the group the first week. Being uncomfortable about being the in-country leader I asked Jose, "Will Hector be the project leader of the team for the entire time the team is in Guatemala?"

Jose nodded and said, "Sure."

I wanted double confirmation and asked again. Jose said, "Yes."

Hector had to return home the morning of the same day Colleen and I arrived. I was shocked to find out that he had left, and I was in charge. I was angry that Jose had lied to me.

Now God had me right where He wanted, feeling totally inadequate through my abilities, and totally dependent on Him. All of our outreach team had done a lot of praying. The Lord helped me overcome my anger, fear, and frustrations. And He told me to listen. I listened for God's wisdom. I listened to my American team who had never seen such poor organization. I listened to the other missionaries who were upset that the Guatemalan pastors and village leaders wouldn't invite us into their churches and villages. I listened to our Guatemalan evangelists who were upset with all of the fighting. I listened to the village pastors who didn't understand why we were there. They asked how we, as outsiders, could help them win their people to Jesus better than they could. It was only after they asked that I shared what the Lord laid on my heart and our vision that would only work if we gave all the glory to God and worked together. Then through the grace of God, He used us to do far more than we could have imagined.

After the outreach project was over, I confronted Jose as to why he had lied.

He said, "I never lied."

I said, "You told me that Hector would be with the team the entire month as the in-country mission leader."

He said, "I never told you that. That was what you wanted to hear, and I just let you believe it."

I said, "I asked you a question that required a yes or no answer. The truth was 'no', but you answered 'yes.' Isn't that a lie?"

He said, "No! I simply let you believe what you wanted to believe. I saw what you were putting together would be a great ministry. I just encouraged you. Look how God used you. Look how everything turned out for the glory of God."

Our "if you are not like me—you are bad dinosaur thinking" clashed. From my culture, I wanted to know the truth and, in reality, if he had told me the truth, the mission project most likely would not have occurred. From his culture, it was okay to bend the truth to encourage me. I was upset because he lied. He was upset because I questioned his honor.

As I look back on that event, I see that God used it to help me mature and to mold me into the person I am today. It taught me to trust the Lord and believe that He is always with me, and He is in control. What God did through us in Guatemala reminded me of *"Now to him who is able to do immeasurably more than all we ask or imagine, according to his power that is at work within us... "(Ephesians 3:20-21).*

Six nights a week we traveled standing in the back of pickup trucks riding to mountain villages. Places that would have taken us four to five hours to walk were an hour bumpy truck ride. When the old truck we had hired broke down, we prayed, "Lord, get us to the villages", and a brand new full-sized pickup truck from a large ranch arrived to take us. Gospel Recordings' messages in local indigenous languages on cassettes were answered prayer in the villages where the literacy rate was only two percent. God blessed our puppet and music ministries and the showing of the Jesus Film. Each night we had two team members give their testimonies. But we always had a local indigenous pastor give the invitation at the end of the film. Our team saw more than 500 decisions to accept Jesus Christ as Lord and Savior, and the membership of many of the local pastors' churches doubled. After we left, the church leaders used the Gospel Recordings' materials we had given them to continue to disciple their new members.

I was walking my prayer walk around the approximately 500 Indians watching the Jesus Film on the last night of our ministry. I noticed that it was raining all around us, but it wasn't raining on the people watching the Jesus Film. We were in the middle of the rainy season where it rains every night, but we never got rained out. Each night God stopped the rain at our location so the tribal people could see and hear about the saving grace of Jesus.

Paul G. Hiebert says in his book titled, *Anthropological Insights for Missionaries*, "Each culture judges values and determines right and wrong. For instance, in North American culture it is worse to tell a lie than to hurt people's feelings. In other cultures, however, it is more important to encourage other people, even if it means bending the truth somewhat." "North Americans assume that honesty means telling people the way things are, even if doing so hurts their feelings. In other countries, it means telling people what they want to hear, for it is more important that they be encouraged than for them to know the truth."[2]

Many American Christians have difficulty understanding that other cultures think differently about the sin of lying. I have had American Christians tell me that Christians should always tell the truth, and telling a lie under any circumstance is wrong. I would like to be a fly on their bedroom walls when their wives ask them, "Does this dress make me look fat?"

The disciples are arguing in Luke 9:46 as to which of them would be the greatest. Their "dinosaur domination, territorialism, and get the mate thinking" was in control of them. At this point Jesus takes a little child to teach the lesson ***"who is the least among you all—he is the greatest." (Luke 9:48b)*** Instead of catching the meaning of what Jesus had just taught, the disciples' "dinosaur thinking" jumped to "if you are not like me—you are bad!"

> *"Master," said John, "we saw a man driving out demons in your name and we tried to stop him, because he is not one of us."*
>
> *"Do not stop him," Jesus said, "for whoever is not against you is for you."*
>
> *As the time approached for him to be taken up to heaven, Jesus resolutely set out for Jerusalem, and he sent messengers on ahead. They went into a Samaritan village to get things ready for him, but the people there did not welcome him, because he was heading for Jerusalem. When the disciples James and John saw this, they asked, "Lord, do you want us to call fire down from heaven to destroy them even as Elijah did?" But Jesus rebuked them, and he said, "You do not know what kind*

of spirit you are of, for the Son of Man did not come to destroy men's lives, but to save them." And they went to another village. (Luke 9:49-56)

Question 2:

Why did John want to stop the man who was driving out demons?

_____

_____

_____

_____

_____

Question 3:

Why did James and John want to destroy the Samaritans?

_____

_____

_____

_____

_____

Because James and John were not Samaritans, the Samaritans did not welcome them. Being rejected hurt and that triggered their "dinosaur hissing" which then triggered their "dinosaur domination thinking" that wanted to destroy the Samaritans.

Question 4:

Why did Jesus stop them and go on to another village?
(Luke 9:56)

_____

_____

_____

_____

_____

_____

_____

_____

_____

The Jews had mistreated the Samaritans for centuries, and it would take a lot of love and caring over a period of time to overcome the bad feelings the Samaritans had. Sending the disciples into the Samaritan village was most likely to teach the disciples. After that lesson, Jesus went to another village.

Question 5:

Do you ever find yourself thinking bad thoughts about people who think differently than you do?

_____

_____

_____

_____

_____

Question 6:

Why did Jonah not want to go to Nineveh?

_____

_____

_____

_____

_____

Jonah hated the people of Nineveh,.because God said they were wicked. (Jonah 1:2) They weren't good like the Israelites. They were bad according to Jonah's "dinosaur thinking." God used Jonah who was convinced that the

Ninevites should be destroyed to convince them to repent of their wickedness and to believe in God.

> **When God saw what they did and how they turned from their evil ways, He had compassion and did not bring upon them the destruction he had threatened.**
>
> **But Jonah was greatly displeased and became angry. He prayed to the Lord, "O Lord, is this not what I said when I was still at home? That is why I was so quick to flee to Tarshish. I knew that you are a gracious and compassionate God, slow to anger and abounding in love, a God who relents from sending calamity. Now, O Lord, take away my life, for it is better for me to die than to live." (Jonah 3:10-4:3)**

Jonah's hatred of the Ninevites was so strong that he would have rather died than see them saved.

A modern day example of "dinosaur if you are not like me—you are bad thinking" is the Fundamental Islamic teaching that all nations are divided into two categories. A nation is either Dar al-Islam, (house of Islam) which is also Dar al-Salam (house at peace) or it is Dar al-Harb, (a territory at war or chaos.) Nations that are under Islamic rule are Dar al–Islam. Nations that are not under Islamic rule are Dar al-Harb.

Question 7:

Does the above fundamental Islamic teaching justify many Christian's dislike and fear of Muslims? Explain your answer.

Remember that the average everyday Muslim is not a theologian, a terrorist, an extremist, or religious. Most Christians in America who fear Muslims haven't known any. We have to be aware of our "if you are not like me—you are bad dinosaur thinking" that can foster hate. Even within Christianity we can have tension between denominations, and Islam has tensions between its sects.

Radical fundamentalists of all types on the extreme ends of religion and politics have a tendency to categorize those in their grouping as "Us," "Good," and "Correct" and others as "Them," "Bad," and "Wrong." Their "if you are not like me—you are bad dinosaur thinking" leads them to believe that those who are outside their position need to be changed, destroyed, or controlled.

Over the last half century a new anti-Christian group has evolved. They are the Secular Fundamentalists, and there may be more of them who are fighting Christian principles and organized religion than there are Muslim terrorists. Their "dinosaur thinking" sees Christians as weak-minded people who need to be controlled. Secular Fundamentalists may have done more to change our lives than terrorists by taking prayer out of school, banning nativity displays on government property, and insisting on what they call political correctness.

Questions 8:

What examples of "if you are not like me—you are bad dinosaur thinking" have you observed?

Question 9:

Have you observed it in your own behavior? How is the Lord leading you to overcome it?

_____

_____

_____

_____

_____

_____

_____

_____

Reflections

"You are my witnesses," declares the Lord, "that I am God." (Isaiah 43:12)

To the weak I became weak, to win the weak. I have become all things to all men so that by all means possible I might save some. (1 Corinthians 9:22)

For the message of the cross is foolishness to those who are perishing, but to us who are being saved it is the power of God. (1 Corinthians 1:18)

"...and with your blood you purchased men for God from every tribe and language and people and nation." (Revelation 5:9)

"Fanatic: A person who's enthusiastic about something in which you have no interest." *Albert Nimeth*

Chapter Nine
FIGHT, FLIGHT, OR FREEZE
(Fear and Worry)

9

God Has Given Us Natural Instincts for Our Physical Protection

This rule is our instinct for physical protection. You experience this when a deer jumps in front of your car. You hit the brakes, and two minutes later you are still clutching the steering wheel. Most threats in our modern world are to our self-esteem. Problems arise when we try to protect the psyche with a system that was designed to protect us from physical danger.

Once when I was walking through some high grass I felt something on my ankle. I looked down, and it was a six foot black snake. I kicked it up in the air and ran. My heart beat fast. I didn't have to think to get away from the snake. My instincts made me. This is the way "fight, flight, or freeze" is supposed to work.

David's Testimony

At this point in the book I'd like to share my testimony of how I accepted Jesus Christ as my Savior. When I was 13 or 14, I occasionally attended church with my grandparents, but I was not always happy about it. I had a temper, swore a lot, and occasionally got into a fight. I believed in God, but I didn't feel that I was good enough to be a Christian because I thought to be a Christian a person had to be really good. However, I liked sports, and our church started a softball team and our assistant pastor was the coach.

At one of our games, a player on the opposing team hit a solid double. However, he tried to make it a triple, and our third baseman had the ball in his glove waiting to tag him out. The runner intentionally ran into our third baseman hitting him hard, trying to be safe by knocking the ball loose. Our coach, the pastor, was up off the bench and onto the field. I can still see the runner's feet going through the air as Coach tossed him and bounced his head a few times off the base bag. Coach swore at him, and the basic translation of what he said was: "If you ever try to hurt one of my boys again, I'll kill you!"

Everyone was shocked thinking, "That man is a pastor!" When he realized what he had done, he apologized to the young man. He went over to the other coach and apologized to him and his team. He then came back to us, and said he was sorry he lost his temper. Then he told us he loved us, and that he would probably do the same thing if he ever saw someone trying to hurt one of us.

That night in my bedroom, I invited Jesus Christ into my heart. I knew my coach was a Christian, and that he loved God and God loved him. Seeing that God could accept him, with a temper, and who sometimes swore, and got into fights, I, for the first time, realized that God could also accept and love me, if I, like my coach, would ask to be forgiven. Through the grace of God I slowly began to change. Now, I don't lose my temper nearly as much, and I seldom swear. But when I do, if I repent, God forgives me. And because I know that I'm not perfect, it is easier for me to forgive others who are also not perfect.

My pastor's beating a person who hurt one of his boys is a good example of the "fight" in "fight, flight, or freeze." He wasn't looking for a fight. His instinctive "fight, flight, or freeze"" was engaged to physically protect a loved one. This is a normal reaction, and you would instantly go into a "fight" mode to protect yourself or a loved one from an attack. This is how God intends for our instincts to protect us from physical danger. But it is not how God wants us to respond to threats to our self-esteem such as someone calling us a bad name.

Deadly Bees

A year or two later I trimmed Christmas trees as a summer job. We trimmed our trees with large machetes, and one day I swung through a hornet's nest cutting it in half. I instantly froze. Within seconds I had hundreds of bees all over me. I knew if I ran or made a sudden movement all of the bees would sting, and I would die. But by instinctively freezing, and then realizing the situation I was in and not moving a muscle, the bees eventually left. It was difficult because I froze with my mouth open, and I had bees on my lips entering and exiting my mouth. If I had shut my mouth I would have been stung. God answered my prayer to not let the bees on my eyes, lips, and tongue bother me which I feel saved my life. Eventually when I thought all of the bees were gone, I slowly started to back away. I praise God that I got away from the bees with only one sting on the back of my ear. This is an example of the "freeze" in "fight, flight, or freeze."

VBS Fiasco

Joy was happy school was out and she had passed first grade, but she was bored with summer vacation. She was excited when her neighbor invited her to go to Vacation Bible School. Joy had never been in a church before. As the bell rang, everyone ran into the classroom and took a seat. Joy took the first seat by the door which the other children intentionally left empty. Joy didn't know that the VBS teacher always chose the person sitting closest to the door to read the first verse from the Bible lesson. She had never heard the Bible read before and was afraid she would embarrass herself by not being able to pronounce the strange words. Joy froze. She couldn't say a word. This was "freeze." At the end of the lesson, the teacher called on Joy to pray as discipline for not taking her turn at reading. The teacher said everyone should know how to pray. But Joy had never heard anyone pray before. As the teacher insisted she pray, Joy ran out of the room screaming, "I want to go home!" This was "flight." Joy didn't come back.

The next day, her neighbor teased her about being afraid to go to church. Joy beat her up. That was "fight."

ATM Mayhem

During the beginning of a summer when Colleen and I had our specialized foster home program, I took two of our boys to the bank to open a savings account. They had just received their first pay check from their summer jobs, and I wanted to teach them how to manage their money. The banker asked them if they wanted an ATM card.

The boys said, "Yes!"

I said, "No! They don't need that temptation. I brought them in to have a simple pass book savings account where it will be a joint account requiring the boy's signature and my signature to make a withdrawal."

The banker said, "I can do that. But the ATM card is the newest thing in banking and makes it real easy for them to have access to their money."

"I don't want it to be easy for them to get at their money. Our goal of opening this…"

The banker interrupted me saying, "The Money Access Card will allow them to withdraw up to $200 out of the ATM machine by just inserting the card and putting in their pin number."

"Look," I said, "I don't want them to have the card. What happens if they take out $200, and they don't have that much in their account?"

The banker said, "We would discover it the next day and call you." (The money access machines were not on line during the early days of ATM.)

I said, "I definitely don't want them to have it. They are not mature enough to handle that responsibility."

The banker said, "The bank feels that way about college students, and they can only withdraw $50. But your boys aren't in college, and there are no restrictions on anyone but college students so they can withdraw the $200."

"You are nuts!" I said. "You are telling me that the bank says college students are only responsible enough to withdraw $50 at a time, but you are allowing adjudicated delinquent high school students to withdraw $200."

The banker continued to defend his territory as the expert banker and said, "The boys don't have to use the cards if you don't want them to. But I'm sure they will eventually want them. I'll just mark the box 'yes.' You can hold the cards until you feel it is okay to give it to them. This way you won't have to make another trip to the bank to order them."

"Please don't do that," I said.

We left the bank with the boys' passbook savings accounts in hand. I never saw the cards in the mail so I assumed the banker did as I requested.

A few weeks later the boys didn't come home on a Friday night. Their natural parents had no idea where they were. I reported them AWOL to their probation officers on Monday morning. Shortly after that the bank called saying both boys had overdrawn their savings account by $800 over the weekend.

The ATM cards were sent, and the boys had taken them out of our mail box without my knowledge. With the ATM cards they decided to go to Florida. Each of the boys withdrew $200 on Friday night and came back shortly after midnight and withdrew $200 more which was posted as a Saturday withdrawal. They laid low and partied all weekend. They came back to the bank late Sunday night and withdrew $200 more and after midnight withdrew another $200 that was posted on Monday. They then hitchhiked to Florida. They had a great time until they ran out of money. The boys then called their parents who advised them to turn themselves in as runaways to the Florida police, and they gave them a free ride home.

Because my name was on the savings account with the boys, a person from the bank called wanting me to give them $1600, $800 for each boy. My "dinosaur fight thinking" was triggered. I went to the bank to give the banker who had given the boys the ATM card over my objections a piece of my mind. I told him the bank should deduct the money from his salary. He said he would talk to the bank VP, and they would write the $1,600 off.

I said, "If you do that how will the boys ever learn to be responsible for their actions?"

The banker said, "It's okay. We have to write off bad loans all the time."

I said, "I want the bank to file charges against the boys. I don't know that they will ever be able to repay the bank, but it is important that the boys realize the seriousness of what they did, and that it was wrong."

The banker said, "If the bank files charges, the judge will laugh me out of court."

"You should be laughed at," I said. "But I'm not concerned about you looking like a fool. I'm concerned about my boys developing responsibly."

The banker's "dinosaur flight thinking" was triggered.

He had the bank write it off so he would not be laughed at. Today, more than thirty years later, his "dinosaur flight thinking" still causes him to avoid me.

The following are sub-rules to "dinosaur fight, flight, or freeze thinking." The purpose of these sub-rules is to protect dinosaur thinkers from ridicule and threats to their self-esteem. The sub-rules are:

- Be perfect
- Be wary, people are out to get you
- Don't trust anyone in authority
- Get even
- Defend yourself
- Protect your tail

The sub-rules protect our "dinosaur thinking" from failure. The "fight" is arguing you are right. The "flight" is running away from responsibility. And, the "freeze" is doing nothing. If you don't do anything, how can you be wrong? [1]

Fear of failure is why many people procrastinate. They want their work to be perfect, and they allow unimportant things to distract them. They subconsciously know perfection is unattainable, and rather than risk ridicule of doing anything wrong, their "dinosaur thinking" creates excuses to justify their inaction. Their self-respect is low because they never accomplish their goals. When they get criticized for not doing what they are supposed to do, they apply the sub-rules of "fight, flight, or freeze."

Most people are afraid to fail. Many won't even try because the fear of failure is so great. When we were in school, most of the questions on the tests we took had only one correct answer. However, in life, there may be different ways to accomplish a goal. It's wise for a person to study the possibilities and take a risk.

Closely tied to this is the sub-rule of "dinosaur, it is mine, thinking" which is "Keep People in Their Place."

People whose "dinosaur thinking" controls their lives never set goals. This leads to a lack of success in their lives. They wander with no direction. They will never hit their target because they don't have one. They lack faith in themselves and in God because they don't see anything good happening to them. When they see good things happen to others, they wish they could be that lucky.

> *"I tell you the truth, if you have faith and do not doubt, not only can you do what was done to the fig tree, but also you can say to this mountain, 'Go, throw yourself into the sea,' and it will be done. If you believe, you will receive whatever you ask for in prayer." (Matthew 21:21-22).*

Earl Nightingale in an audio recording says that 27% of the people in the USA have no idea what they are going to do during the day when they wake up in the morning, 57% of the people wake up knowing what they don't want to do, and 16% wake up knowing what they want to do that day. Of the 16%, only 3% are directed towards a life goal.

Marsha Sinetar in her book, <u>Do What</u> You Love, the Money Will Follow, says 85% of American workers dislike their jobs. She also says the highest paid people in any profession are those who love their work. People who love what they do ultimately become the best in their fields.

Little Bitty Frying Pan

Zig Zigler in an audio recording tells the story about Gentleman Jim Corbett, the former heavyweight boxing champion. Corbett was jogging around a lake one day, and noticed a fisherman who was catching all kinds of fish. This fisherman was doing the craziest thing—throwing the big fish back and keeping the small ones. Each time Corbett jogged by, he couldn't believe what he saw.

Finally, Corbett runs to the fisherman and says, "I've never seen anybody like you catching all kinds of fish. You keep the little ones and throw back the big ones. Man, that is crazy! Why in the world would you do that?"

The fisherman showed Corbett his frying pan and said, "All I have is this little bitty frying pan."

Have you ever shared an idea you had with a friend or family member only to be told it would never work? Telling a person his ideas are no good is telling him to be content with his little bitty frying pan.

Often in my *Help For Parents* Workshops, I asked parents to share the last great idea they had. Afterwards, I asked what their friends and family said about their ideas. Over 90% of the time, their ideas were put down and discouraged. I've discovered about half the people over 40 can't remember ever having a great idea. What happens far too often in our society is we stop dreaming as we age. We become conditioned to stay in our place.

Have you ever seen a flea circus? You can train fleas by putting them in a covered jar. The first hour you hear a continual light tapping from the fleas jumping and hitting the lid. As time passes, you hear the fleas hitting the lid less and less. Finally you can take the lid off. The fleas are physically able to jump out, but they won't because they think they can't.

What would happen to our children if they heard, "That would be great!" instead of "You could never do that." Maybe we could say, "What are you going to have to do to accomplish that?" Then follow up with "Good. Let's get started."

What would our self-respect be if we were surrounded by positive people who believed we could do anything we put our minds to?

Susan Jeffers in her audio, *Feel the Fear and Do It Anyway* identifies five truths about fear.

Truth #1: **Fear will never go away as long as you continue to grow.** Most people don't like hearing this. It would be nice if there were magical advice that would make our fears go away, but there isn't. Now you can be relieved that you no longer have to work so hard to get rid of your fear because it isn't going to go away. Fear is natural for all of us every time we attempt something new.

Truth #2: **The only way to get rid of the fear of doing something is to go out and do it.** This may sound contradictory to truth # 1. Fear of particular situations will dissolve when we confront them. You have to act. The doing it comes before the fear goes away. But if we wait for our fears to go away, we may never do anything.

Truth #3: **The only way to feel better about yourself is to go out and do it.** Many people say, "When I feel better about myself, I'll do it." But again, it doesn't work that way. You have to act before you feel better. When you make something happen, not only does the fear of that situation leave, you also do a lot towards building your self-confidence.

Truth #4: **Everyone experiences fear on unfamiliar territory.** That means all those people you envy for not being afraid have been afraid. You are not alone.

The person controlled by his "dinosaur thinking" says, "Why should I put myself through all the discomfort that comes with taking risks? I'll just live my life the way I've been living it." But the person who has overcome his "dinosaur thinking" understands the next truth.

Truth #5: **Pushing through fear is less frightening than living with the bigger fear that comes from a feeling of helplessness.** The more helpless a person feels, the more severe is the undercurrent of dread that comes with knowing there are situations in life over which he has no control. You have no control over things such as the loss of a spouse, parent, or child, or the loss of a job. The dinosaur thinker obsesses about possible catastrophes. He says, "What if…" Fear permeates his life. The irony is that people who refuse to take risks live with a feeling of dread that is far more severe than what they would feel if they took the risks necessary to make themselves less helpless.

The person who is afraid to take risks feels he is a victim. He worries and feels helpless to do anything about his situation. But the person who feels the fear and does what he has to do, develops a greater sense of worth and self-control.

Fear is a strong emotion. (Whenever fear and logic are considered in making a decision, fear always wins.) You have no control over your fear, but you do have control over your actions. Don't worry about being afraid, just do it. Over 90 percent of what people worry about never happens. You will feel much better if you just do it as compared to how you'll feel if you worry yourself into inaction.

When an animal is stimulated, its instinct determines its response. But with man, a choice lies between the stimulus and the response. You may not be in control of what happens to you, but you are in control of how you react. You don't have to fight. You don't have to run. You don't have to freeze. You can choose to do what needs to be done.

Colonel Sanders

Tony Robbins in his audio program, *Unlimited Power*, tells about Colonel Sanders, the founder of the Kentucky Fried Chicken franchise. This is an illustration of a man who overcame his "fight, flight, or freeze dinosaur thinking." When the Colonel turned 65, he received his first social security check in the amount of $99. Looking at it, he decided he wasn't going to live like that. He wanted more than to simply exist. He decided to earn some extra money from his popular chicken recipe.

Colonel Sanders made his first sales call on a small restaurant and offered his terrific chicken recipe to the restaurant owner. It wouldn't cost the owner a cent. All the restaurant owner had to do was pay Colonel Sanders a small percentage of the increased profits as a result of using his recipe. The restaurant owner said, "No!" He already had a chicken recipe. For most people with an idea that would have been the end of it. But Colonel Sanders kept making sales calls. He even slept in his car as he traveled across the USA.

The Colonel kept notes and every time he got a rejection, he wrote down exactly what he did, made some alterations in his sales pitch, and tried again. He learned from each failure, and never gave up. On his 1,010th sales call, Colonel Sanders received his first yes.

Colonel Sanders believed in his recipe and his idea. After 1,009 people had said no, he was still asking. Many people with an idea are afraid to ask even once. The majority of people stop trying with their first rejection. Our fear of failure keeps us from trying. Many great businessmen have gone bankrupt several times before they finally made it.

Edison, in inventing the light bulb, said, "I never failed. I discovered over 10,000 ways of how not to make a light bulb." The truth is, if we are open-minded and not afraid to fail, we can learn from every situation that doesn't work the way we hoped. We can make adjustments and try again and again until we finally succeed. It has been said that genius is one percent inspiration and 99 percent perspiration. But the dinosaur thinker avoids what is hard and necessary. He prefers blaming, complaining, and protecting his tail. His fear of failure makes him avoid accepting responsibility or taking risks.

The 'Fun–er–al'

"Fight, flight, or freeze dinosaur thinking" causes many people to worry.

Back when I was a pastor, I frequently called on Mae, an elderly lady whose husband had died. She was having a rough time and complained, "Why is God punishing me?" I would tell her, "God isn't punishing you. It is not about you. Life is life, and death is part of it. God is calling us to trust, love, and be obedient to Him in all circumstances. He is in control."

The thing Mae worried most about was her funeral. She had written down the hymns she wanted sung and the Scripture she wanted me to read. She wanted to make sure I mentioned her grandchildren and great grandchildren by name and tell each of them that Grandma loved them. She worried about where to keep the paper with all this information so when she died I would get it to prepare for her funeral. She would forget where she put it and cry about it when I visited. She didn't want to give the paper to me for fear of thinking of something new to add.

Mae was too frail to come to church so the church recorded all of the services for her. I announced to the church on a communion Sunday that all of Mae's family was visiting, and I was going to stop over after the service to give her communion. I invited anyone who would like to come to join me. About ten people came.

Mae was full of joy with all of her friends and family with her. Then she thought of something she wanted to add to her funeral list. She couldn't remember where she put it, and she started to cry. I prayed, "Lord, help me deal with this lady." The craziest idea came to my mind. It had to be the Holy Spirit. I said, "Mae, you don't have to be worried about your funeral service. You have done so much planning and work on it and when we have it you will be dead and won't be even able to enjoy it. Isn't everyone here that you want to be at your funeral?"

She looked around and said, "Yes."

I said, "Do you know the term funeral is not listed in my worship book?" I showed her the appendix and said, "What you call funeral is listed as 'Witness to the Resurrection.' Now funeral is spelled FUN-ER-AL. Let's pronounce it fun-er-all. At your funeral you will be lying there dead, and everyone in this house will walk past your casket and lie saying, "Doesn't she look good?" They will tell your daughter and grandchildren how they remembered you, and you won't be able to hear or respond to what they say. So at this 'fun er all' you are alive! Let's have everyone line up and walk by you. Each one can tell you what they remember most about you, and you will hear it and be able to tell them what you remember most about them. Doesn't a 'fun er all' sound better than a funeral? And after the 'fun er all' you won't have to worry about what you want me to say at your funeral because you would have already said it."

She was excited. All of her grandchildren went to her one at a time and said, "Grandma, I love you." She hugged and kissed them and told each one of them why he/she was special. Then she continued telling each neighbor and friend and lastly her daughter. It was one of the most beautiful things I had ever seen.

I said, "Everyone has seen you now. Wasn't that nicer than waiting until you're dead?" We then sang "Jesus Loves Me" and after we finished singing I said, "Mae, when I do your service I would like to share with everyone there that we know for sure that you are going to Heaven. Do you know for sure that you are going to Heaven when you die?"

She said, "I think so."

I said, "Do you want to know for sure?"

She said, "Yes."

I said, "It is as easy as ABC."

She smiled and said, "I remember you preaching on this. I taught school for thirty years, and now I'm going to say my ABC's."

I said, "(A) Mae do you accept that you are you a sinner?"

She started to cry, and said, "I am a sinner. I worry too much."

After she calmed down I said, "(B) Do you believe that Jesus Christ died for your sins?"

She said, "Jesus died for my sins, and I believe in my heart and I (C), confess with my mouth that Jesus is Lord. And it is my prayer for everyone here that you will all be saved."

The entire room rejoiced and cried. We followed that with the communion service which was why I went there in the first place.

Do Not Worry

"Therefore I tell you, do not worry about your life, what you will eat or drink; or about your body, what you will wear. Is not life more important than clothes? Look at the birds of the air; they do not sow or reap or store away in barns, and yet your heavenly Father feeds them. Are you not much more valuable than they? Who of you by worrying can add a single hour to his life?"

"And why do you worry about clothes? See how the lilies of the field grow. They do not labor or spin. Yet I tell you that not even Solomon in all his splendor was dressed like one of these. If that is how God clothes the grass of the field, which is here today and tomorrow is thrown into the fire, will he not much more clothe you, O you of little faith? So do not worry, saying, 'What shall we eat?' or 'What shall we wear?' For the pagans run after all these things, and your heavenly Father knows you need them. But seek first his kingdom and his righteousness, and all these things will be given to you as well." (Matthew 6:25-33)

Question 1:
Is worrying a sin?

Jesus tells us not to worry, and if we do something Jesus tells us not to do, that is a sin. But we know through Adam that we all have a sinful nature, so worrying is part of that.

Question 2:

Is worrying proof that you do not really trust God?

_____

_____

_____

_____

We need to confess our worrying as a sin and pray as the man who asked Jesus to heal his son in (**Mark 9:24.**) *"I do believe, help me overcome my unbelief."*

Question 3:

What is your thought on the following statement? "Most Christians believe in God, but don't believe God."

_____

_____

_____

_____

_____

_____

A person can believe in God without believing that God will do what He says He will do and without trusting Him. Many people are afraid to truly give everything to Him and live the way the Bible says we should live.

Question 4:

Are you afraid to really believe God? Why or why not?

_____

_____

_____

_____

_____

Question 5:

Have you observed "dinosaur, fight, flight, or freeze, thinking" reactions to the church? Explain.

_____

_____

_____

_____

_____

A "fight" reaction with "dinosaur domination thinking" is what we may see in Secular Fundamentalists. They reject Christ's teaching because they don't want to submit to the ultimate authority of God. Because they feel their thinking has evolved to a higher level than Christianity, they are threatened by the thought that God is truth. They are trying to destroy Christianity's influence on society through judicial and political means.

A "flight" reaction to Jesus may be what we see in people who grew up in the church, yet don't attend when they become adults. Many of these people feel that church is not relevant to them anymore. They stay away because they don't want to submit to a higher authority that could cramp their life style.

A "freeze" reaction may be what we see when people are invited to come to church and don't come. They may be afraid of what would happen if they gave their lives to Christ.

Question 6:

What is the best way to witness to people who may have "fight, flight, or freeze" responses to Christ?

The best way to witness is to be a Christian who puts Christ first. You need to be a model of a life that believes God and trusts Him.

Stress

We are a restless people obsessed and anxious about many things. We have even coined a term, "stress," to describe this condition. We can blame a fumbling young researcher named Hans Selye for introducing us to stress. Selye had a bad habit of accidently dropping his lab rats, then chasing them around the room, and finally trapping them beneath a sink. When they developed ulcers and shrunken immune tissues, Selye did some tests and realized what was happening: His clumsiness was making them sick. Searching for a word to describe this response of life under tension, Selye borrowed a term from engineering and "stress" was born.[2]

Stress may be killing more of the world's population than AIDS. About 25 million Americans are thought to have hypertension, although half don't know they have it. Stress is frequently found as the major cause of respiratory infections, arthritis, colitis, asthma, uneven heart rhythms, many sexual problems, circulatory problems, and even cancer. The doctors of the American Academy of Psychosomatic Medicine believe that 75 to 90 percent of all reported diseases are due in part to stress. The three best selling prescription drugs in America are Prozac and its derivatives for relaxation, Inderal for high blood pressure, and Tagamet for ulcers. Leaders in the industry estimate that 50 to 75 billion dollars are lost each year due to stress-related symptoms. Stress takes a heavy toll.[3]

Even if our health is not at risk, certainly our peace of mind is. We're like that couple who had their home broken into. The husband heard a noise in the middle of the night. He went downstairs to investigate and found a burglar. He said to the man, "Stay where you are. I want to get my wife. She has been expecting you for twenty years."

When we are fearful, our "dinosaur thinking" won't let us genuinely share our resources. We view the world with a deep seated scarcity as if there weren't enough love, money, praise, and attention to go around. You must overcome this and the rest of your "dinosaur thinking" to become the person God intends for you to be. Scripture says, ***"But thanks be to God, who always leads us in triumphal procession in Christ and through us spreads everywhere the fragrance of the knowledge of Him." (2 Cor. 2:14)*** You may think overcoming your "dinosaur thinking" and fears is hard. But God has designed you to triumph. You cannot triumph unless you have been through the battle.

Reflections

Be strong and courageous. Do not be terrified; do not be discouraged, for the Lord your God will be with you wherever you go. (Joshua 1:9)

"A ship in harbor is safe, but that is not what ships are built for." *William Shedd*

"Don't allow fear of the unknown to cause you to miss out on what God wants to do through you. Worse than failure is living with the regret of never having stepped out in faith to pursue your vision." *Andy Stanley*

"Do the thing you fear and the death of fear is certain." *Ralph Waldo Emerson*

"Forsake your wimp factor, take a step and be proactive." *George Verwer*

"I am looking for a lot of men who have an infinite capacity to not know what can't be done." *Henry Ford*

Chapter Ten

OVERCOMING OUR DINOSAUR THINKING BY GIVING

The Dinosaur Thinker Doesn't Know How to Give

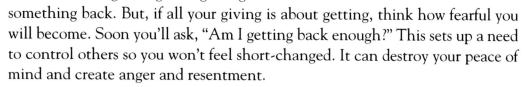

Most people would say that they are giving. But are they? All too often, they exchange a "You do that for me," for a "Then I'll do this for you." That is a hidden barter system where they don't give anything without expecting something in return. There is nothing wrong with getting something back. But, if all your giving is about getting, think how fearful you will become. Soon you'll ask, "Am I getting back enough?" This sets up a need to control others so you won't feel short-changed. It can destroy your peace of mind and create anger and resentment.

As babies, we are the personification of neediness. We come into the world as total takers. We have to take, or we will die. Our survival is tied up with the world nurturing us. As the years pass, we function more and more as independent beings able to take care of ourselves. Yet the "dinosaur thinking" part of us never develops beyond the crib. It remains frightened that no one will come to relieve its hunger.

One thing that will help overcome "dinosaur thinking" is to develop a program of giving. Start giving thanks, help, information, time, and love. Start thanking people for the things they do for you. Look for ways to help the people around you. Share information that will help others. Take time to listen and show you care. Start saying thank you, thank you, thank you. Start giving "Thank Yous" away instead of waiting for them to come to you. The trick to receiving blessings from your relationships isn't figuring out how to get more. It is figuring out how you can give more.

The Irish Hitchhiker

Back in the early 1970's, I picked up a hitchhiker outside of Pittsburgh as I was returning to graduate school in Philadelphia. The hitchhiker was 19 years old, about six feet tall, weighed 230 pounds, and was dressed like he was a deckhand on a freight ship. After he threw his bags in the back of my pickup and climbed into the cab, I asked, "Where are you going?"

He answered, "Ireland, but I have to go to New York or Philadelphia first to find a job on a freighter going back to England."

I said, "I'm going to Philadelphia."

He said, "That would be fine."

I said, "I don't know that I have ever met a real live Irishman before. What brought you to America?"

"My uncle has a farm in Iowa," he said. "I worked my way from Ireland to New York on a freighter and hitchhiked from New York to Iowa to reach my uncle's. I worked for him all summer and now that the crops are harvested, I'm returning home to go to school."

"I have to ask you a question," I said. "With you being from Ireland and all of the reports we get in the news about the fighting between the Catholics and Protestants, which are you, a Catholic or a Protestant?"

He replied, "I'm an Atheist. In Ireland, that is the safest thing to be. I can't believe in a God who could allow two people who both claim to believe in Him to hate and kill each other."

I learned a lot over the next couple of hours. This young man told me about his first-hand accounts where he had seen bombings, and witnessed the killing of

Catholics, Protestants, and soldiers. Police and soldiers had frisked him multiple times. He shared some deep hurts with me because I showed him I cared by listening and asking questions.

He finally decided it was time to change the subject and coming back to my original question, asked me, "Which are you, Catholic or Protestant?"

I said, "I am a Protestant, but I like to think of myself first as a Christian rather than as a member of a denomination of Christians."

Over the next hour he learned a lot from me as I answered his many questions. As we approached Philadelphia, he started to study a map of the city and pointed to the place he wanted to be dropped off.

"I'm not dropping you off there," I exclaimed. "It wouldn't be safe for you to walk through that neighborhood, plus it is starting to rain. I'll just take you down and drop you off at the shipyard."

"Oh no," he said. "I'm not having you go out of your way for me."

"What do you mean go out of my way? It would at most be only a half hour. I've enjoyed your company and want to get you safely to where you are going," I said.

He raised his voice, "NO! I'm not having you go out of your way for me."

I pulled the truck over to the side of the road and said, "If you won't let me take you downtown, at least let me drop you at a place that will be safe and easy for you to get there. Let me look at that map."

I spotted a subway station where I could drop him off and showed it to him on the map. I said, "Let me drop you off here. I'm actually going right by it anyway." I'm sure God has forgiven me for telling that lie.

He started to cry as I pulled over at the entrance. I asked, "What's the matter? Do you have enough money?" I pulled $20 from my wallet and tried to give it to him.

He cried all the more and refused to take any money.

I didn't know what to do but sit there and pray silently that God would help him and show me what to say or do.

As he dried his eyes, he said, "No one has ever done anything for me in my entire life who has not expected me to do something in return. I've never met anyone like you. I've told you things that I've never told anyone before.

You've gone out of your way to get me here. You have offered me money. I don't even know your name, and I'll never see you again. There is no way I can ever pay you back."

I interrupted him saying, "I didn't do anything special."

"No," he said. "Let me finish. I've never believed in God. I've never known anyone who claimed to be a Protestant or Catholic who lived a life that I would want to believe in their God. If I ever believe in God, I want to believe like you and believe in the God you believe in."

The Only Thing I Have Kept Is What I Gave Away

Early in the twentieth century a man gave $100,000 to build a college in Liberia. By the 1940's the college had grown, and had educated thousands of young Africans. On an anniversary of the college's founding, the administration decided it was time to say "Thank You" to its benefactor. It took months to track him down. The man had lost everything in the stock market crash of 1929, and was living in a little house on the south side of Chicago. Twice he refused to see the representatives from the college, but finally he agreed to receive them. At their insistence he was flown to Africa for the celebration. As he looked over the campus filled with hundreds of students, he whispered to the college president, "The only thing I have kept is what I gave away." Only what we give away is ours forever. [1]

Reflections

Bring the whole tithe into the storehouse, that there may be food in my house. Test me in this," says the Lord Almighty, "and see if I will not throw open the flood gates of heaven and pour out so much blessing that you will not have room enough for it. (Malachi 3:10)

Give, and it will be given to you. A good measure, pressed down, shaken together and running over, will be poured into your lap. For with the measure you use, it will be measured to you.(Luke 6:38)

*Each man should give what he has decided in his heart to give, not reluc-
tantly or under compulsion, for God loves a cheerful giver.(2 Corinthians 9:7)*

"You can give without loving, but you cannot love without giving." *Amy
Carmichael*

"You do not test the resources of God until you attempt the impossible."
F. B. Meyer

"I never knew a child of God bankrupted by his benevolence. What we keep
we may lose, but what we give to Christ we are sure to keep." *Theodore L. Cuyler*

"Do you realize that you and I are God's gift to the world?" *Josh McDowell*

"Consistent giving strengthens the heart, tones the wallet and exercises your
faith." *Dave Davidson*

"Generosity increases our joy because it frees us. It releases us from the grip of
money because we have the courage to give it away. In days of economic uncer-
tainty, many spend precious emotional energy worrying about the future. They
fear either not getting what they want or losing what they have. Generosity puts
our lives in a wider arena. We take our eyes off ourselves and realize that God is
our provider, and He will take care of us." *Paul Borthwick*

Chapter Eleven
LIVING FOR JESUS

Revealing What God Wants of Us

All Christians would love to receive God's blessings. We pray God gives us a good education. We hope and pray we find the prefect mate, and/or our marriage will be blessed. We ask God to bless us in our work and finances and to give us a nice home. We want to attend a good church where the preaching and adult programs challenge us with the Word of God and are relevant in our lives. We want our church to have good music (the kind we like), and good Sunday School and programs for our children. All of the above are good. It is like we want to enter into a contract with Jesus where we tell Him our plans for our lives and

```
┌─────────────────────────────────┐
│           MY PLAN               │
│                                 │
│  School:                        │
│                                 │
│                                 │
│  Marriage:                      │
│                                 │
│                                 │
│  Career:                        │
│                                 │
│                                 │
│  Home:                          │
│                                 │
│                                 │
│  Church:                        │
│                                 │
│         _____        │
│                  Jesus Christ   │
└─────────────────────────────────┘
```

have Him sign His approval on them. (Like the contract of the outline on the previous page filled out with our desires.)

There is nothing wrong with anything we want in this contract. However, wanting that type of relationship with God is not biblical. It is "dinosaur thinking" and self-centeredness.

The disciples often thought this way in their early walk with Jesus. After James and John's mother asked Him to grant them high positions in the kingdom, He said,

> *"You know that the rulers of the Gentiles lord it over them, and their high officials exercise authority over them. Not so with you. Instead, whoever wants to become great among you must be your servant, and whoever wants to be first must be your slave—just as the Son of Man did not come to be served, but to serve, and to give his life as a ransom for many." (Matthew 20:25-28)*

Jesus took off His outer garments and washed the disciples' feet immediately after serving them the Last Supper. He knew that it would be His last teaching opportunity with them before He would be crucified.

Do you think what Jesus taught there might be important?

When He had finished washing their feet, He put on His clothes and returned to His place.

> *"Do you understand what I have done for you?" he asked them. "You call me 'Teacher' and 'Lord,' and rightly so, for that is what I am. Now that I, your Lord and Teacher, have washed your feet, you also should wash one another's feet. I have set you an example that you should do as I have done for you. I tell you the truth, no servant is greater than his master, nor is a messenger greater than the one who sent him. Now that you know these things, you will be blessed if you do them." (John 13:12-17)*

Forty days after the resurrection, the disciples still hadn't totally overcome their "dinosaur thinking" and asked Jesus just before He ascended, **"Lord, are you at this time going to restore the kingdom to Israel?"(Acts 1:6b)**

Jesus said to them: *"It is not for you to know the times or the dates the Father has set by His own authority. But you will receive power when the Holy Spirit comes on you to be my witnesses in Jerusalem, and all Judea and Samaria, and to the ends of the earth." (Acts:7-8)*

This was the last thing Jesus said to them, and he wanted to get their attention, so as soon as he said it, he ascended up to Heaven.

Do you think what He said there might be really important?

Jesus wants to bless you with the power of the Holy Spirit so you can be a witness. Jesus' goal in blessing you is not that you just get blessed. His goal in blessing you is to empower you with the Holy Spirit so you can serve others which will make you a witness for Him.

The type of contract that biblically reflects the relationship Jesus wants you to have with Him is as follows.

GOD'S PLAN FOR MY LIFE

_____
My Signature

Yes, the contract is blank. God wants you to give Him your life with no preconditions. Are you willing to accept Jesus Christ as Lord and Master of your life, to no longer merely include God in your plans, but to want God to include you in His plan, whatever that means, whatever the cost, ANYTHING, ANY TIME, ANYWHERE?

Reflections

"...If anyone would come after me, he must deny himself and take up his cross daily and follow me." (Luke 9:23)

"Multitudes, multitudes in the valley of decision! For the day of the Lord is near in the valley of decision." (Joel 3:14)

"Look at the nations and watch- and be utterly amazed: For I am going to do something in your days that you would not believe, even if you were told." (Habakkuk 1:5)

"...The harvest is plentiful, but the workers are few. Ask the Lord of the harvest, therefore to send out workers into his harvest field." (Luke 10:2)

"Now all has been heard; here is the conclusion of the matter: Fear God and keep his commandments, for this is the whole duty of man." (Ecclesiastes 12:13)

"God always gives his best to those who leave the choice to Him."   *Jim Elliot*

Could a mariner sit idle
   If he heard the drowning cry?
Could a doctor sit in comfort
   And just let his patients die?
Could a fireman sit idle,
   Let men burn and give no hand?
Can you sit at ease in Zion
   With unreached peoples damned?
      ~*Leonard Ravenhill*

"Your mission, if you decide to accept it, is an exciting, adventurous abundant life with almighty God as your very own personal guide in following His plan, on His terms, with His power." *Dave Davidson*

CONCLUSION

At the last great council of the dinosaurs, they all voted not to change. That is why they became extinct. They wanted to keep everything in its place. Today, dinosaur thinkers are still afraid of change.

There are only three things that do not change. The first thing that never changes is God. ***"Jesus Christ is the same yesterday and today and forever." (Hebrews 13:8)*** The second thing that never changes is God's law and the principles of Godly integrity that come from the Bible. The only other thing that never changes is that everything else keeps changing. Simply stated, God and His principles do not change in a changing world.

It is only through Jesus Christ that you can overcome your "dinosaur thinking" and make the changes in your life to become the person God intends for you to be. You can't overcome it on your own because "dinosaur thinking" is sin which is the opposite of love.

Many people think the opposite of love is hate. It is not. The opposite of love is self-love. It is putting ourselves and our desires ahead of God and everyone else. People, controlled by "dinosaur thinking," always put themselves first. That is why we dominate, blame others, argue, are jealous, greedy, and prideful. It is why we are impatient, blaming, complaining, and refusing to accept responsibility. It is why we have difficulties in our marriages and relationships and think less of others who aren't like us. It is our "dinosaur thinking" that makes us want to control everything. And when we can't, we are afraid.

The Apostle Paul summed up the sinful nature of "dinosaur thinking" when he said:

> *"The acts of the sinful nature are obvious: sexual immorality, impurity and debauchery; idolatry and witchcraft; hatred, discord, jealousy, fits of rage, selfish ambition, dissensions,*

factions and envy; drunkenness, orgies and the like." (Galatians 4:19-21a)

You can't overcome your "dinosaur thinking" on your own. True joy comes from accepting you are a sinner in need of Jesus Christ, believing in Him as your Lord and Savior, and calling on Him. We are saved not by our works, but by His grace.

Jesus wants you to open your heart to Him and pray the way He taught the disciples, *"Your (God's) kingdom come, Your (God's) will be done on earth as it is in heaven." (Matthew 6:10)* When you pray this way, He wants to bless you with the fruit of the Spirit which is *"love, joy, peace, patience, kindness, goodness, faithfulness, gentleness and self-control." (Galatians 5:22-23a)*

You need these gifts to become the person God intends for you to be.

Jesus also wants you to pray, *"Give us today our daily bread." (Matthew 6:11)* This is not just praying for food. Jesus said, *"I am the bread of Life." (John 6:35)* He wants you to pray that He will be in you as He prayed for you and all believers the night before He went to the cross, *"That all of them (believers) may be one, Father, just as You are in Me and I am in You. May they also be in us so that the world may believe that You sent Me." (John 17:21)* When you pray this way, God wants to bless you so He can use you to be a blessing to others. In this process, God will give you a passion to start being that special person that can do that special work He wants for you to do.

I praise God that He works through me in my writing and presenting "Overcoming Dinosaur Thinking" workshops and seminars. My prayer is that this work has helped you find the secret of right relationships and has been a blessing to you so God will be glorified as He uses you to be a blessing to others.

END NOTES

Chapter Two, DOMINATION—Part Two

1   Anonymous, *London Times,*

2   www.answers.com/topicbarbary-pirate-1
         & www.columbia.edu/cu/news/05/11/michaelOren.html

Chapter Three, TERRITORIALISM (It's Mine!)

1   www.worldmapper.org/

Chapter Four, I WANT IT NOW (I Want It Now!)—Part One

1   Bernstein and Rozen, *Dinosaur Brains, Dealing with All Those Impossible People at Work.* Nightingale-Conant Audio, 1989

2   Earl Nightengale, *Insight* audio magazine

3   Steven Covey, *Seven Habits of Highly Effective People,* New York, Simon & Schuster Audio, 2002

Chapter Five, I WANT IT NOW (I Want It Now!)—Part Two

1   Ray Comfort, *Hell's Best Kept Secret,* 1982

Chapter Six, BLAMING AND COMPAINING (Hissing)

1   Dale Losch, State of the Universe Address, Cross World, 2008

2   Bishop Stanley K. Smith, Brown Bag Bible Study, Meadville, PA, St. John Full Gospel Missionary Baptist Church, 2011

Chapter Seven, TWISTING THE TRUTH (Get the Mate)

1   Glenn J. Schwartz, *When Charity Destroys Dignity*, World Mission Associates, 2008

Chapter Eight, JUDGING OTHERS (If You Are Not Like Me—You Are Bad)

1   Bernstein and Rozen, *Dinosaur Brains*, Nightingale-Conant Audio, 1989

2   Paul G. Hiebert, *Anthropological Insights for Missionaries*, Baker, 1986

Chapter Nine, FIGHT, FLIGHT, or FREEZE (Fear and Worry)

1   Bernstein and Rozen, *Dinosaur Brains*, Nightingale-Conant Audio, 1989

2   Barbara Paulson, "A Nation out of Balance," *HEALTH*, October 1994,

3   John Powell, Happiness Is an Inside Job, Tabor Publishing, 1989

Chapter Ten, OVERCOMING DINOSAUR THINKING by GIVING

1   King Duncan, "Three Foolish Things You can Do With Your Money," *Dynamic Preaching*, August 1995

BIBLIOGRAPHY

T his bibliography is my attempt to give credit to speakers and authors whose books and audio programs have blessed me over the years and helped me develop many of the concepts I use in this book. Forgive me if I've left some out.

Albert Bernstein & Sydney Craft Rozen, *Dinosaur Brains, Dealing With All Those Impossible People at Work*, Chicago, Nightingale-Conant Audio, March 1990

Ray Comfort, *Hell's Best Kept Secret*, New Kensington, PA, Whitaker House, 1989

Steve Corbett & Brain Fikkert, *WHEN HELPING HURTS, How to Alleviate Poverty Without Hurting the Poor and Yourself, Chicago*, Moody, 2009

Steven Covey, *Seven Habits of Highly Effective People*, New York, Simon & Schuster Audio, 2002

Dan & David Davidson & George Verwer, *God's Great Ambition*, Fort Worth, Authentic, 2001

William Easum, *Dancing with Dinosaurs, Ministry in a Hostile & Hurting World*, Nashville, Abington Press, 1993

Suzette Haden Elgin, *Mastering The Gentle Art of Verbal Self-Defense*, Upper Saddle River, NJ, Prentice Hall Audio, 1989

Paul G. Hiebert, *Anthropological Insights for Missionaries*, Alda, MI, Baker, 1986

Susan Jeffers, *Feel the Fear and Do It Anyway*, Englewood Cliffs, NJ, Simon & Shuster Audio, 2001

Dale Losch, State of the Universe Address, Washington Bible College, Cross World, 2009

Tony Robbins, *Unlimited Power*, Chicago, Nightingale-Conant Audio, 1989

Glenn J. Schwartz, *When Charity Destroys Dignity, Lancaster*, World Mission Associates, 2008

Marsha Sinetar, *Do What You Love, The Money Will Follow*, New York, Simon & Schuster Audio, 2005

Bishop Stanley K. Smith, Brown Bag Bible Study, Meadville, PA, St. John Full Gospel Baptist Missionary Church, 2011

Zig Ziglar, Goals, Chicago, Nightingale-Conant Audio, 2001

A Testimony of David Derby's Work in India

Often men are ignorant of divine things, and believe everything with their unstable faith. It is not easy to teach them. Only those who are thoroughly instructed in whatsoever Christ has commanded can be considered as proper teachers of the ignorant, and Dr. David Blair Derby is one of them. (Doctor is an honorary title bestowed on Rev. Derby by many tribal Christians in India.) He has spared several months between 2008 and 2010 from his busy schedule visiting eastern and northern India. He taught more than 1,000 people (mostly grass roots level Christian workers and lay leaders of whom many were illiterate.) He communicated the Biblical truth in a simple manner. Those who attended his workshop tell me how his teaching helped them to learn and practice divine truth in their lives, and then in their families, and congregations.

I have seen people who attended Dr. Derby's training use his Indian edition of this book as a text book for Sunday school classes, weekly Bible studies, and even youth meetings. I praise the Lord that this book is available in several Indian languages. This is really helpful for those of differing languages, and we pray for translation in several other Indian languages.

I was privileged to accompany Dr. Derby on these workshops which were indeed blessings for our work in Global Recordings Network—India. I was able to talk with many of the participants who gave me reliable information about their languages, cultures, need for the field, etc. I was able to find good contacts through the workshops and praise God that I found language helpers to make and provide recordings to the unreached language groups of—BHOJPURI, MAITHILI, MAGAHI, SAURA LANGIYA, KUI and SAURA ORISSA. I am thankful to God for Dr. Derby as he has provided funds towards the recordings and distribution in all the above languages. Because of it, I completed the work in time and sent gospel outreach CDs to the above language groups, and people are now listening to those every day in their own languages. Many non-Christians have started to join in the church service and are asking for prayer and God's blessing. This is the result of Dr. Derby's work.

Praise God for the call Dr. Derby has to live for Christ's sake, and to teach Christians all that Christ has taught to make them good disciples. We are saddened that the immigration authorities in India have banned him from returning, but praise God that He is multiplying the Indian missionaries who have been empowered by Dr. Derby's love of God and his vision. We are amazed that God has multiplied the outreach of Dr. Derby's work through being denied entry to India.

At last, I join with all the participants and pray that the Divine favor of Jesus be on Dr. Derby and this book. We know it will bless you as it has us, and a portion of the proceeds of this book's sales will go to assist us in our partnerships to provide the resources needed to reach all of the Unreached Peoples of India.

Swapan Roy
Field Executive & Senior Audio Technician, GRN—India
Disciples for the Harvest—India, Volunteer

David Derby is the founder and director of the Disciples for the Harvest project, in partnership with Advancing Native Missions. The goal of Disciples for the Harvest is to train an army of disciples who will be obedient to the Great Commission. Through the grace of God, David, with the help of his indigenous Indian ministry and mission partners, has trained more than 1,000 grass root level church planters and Christian leaders throughout eight states in India between 2008 and 2010. David was denied entry into India in 2011. But we serve a mighty God who used that event to multiply the work being done.

You can make a tax deductible donation to continue the momentum of the work that God is doing through India's grass root level pastors and missionaries who are continuing the work, by sending your check to:

ANM
P.O. Box 5303
Charlottesville, VA 22905

Please attach a note saying,
"For Disciples for the Harvest—Account 600DFH"
to your donation.

Notes

The SECRET of RIGHT RELATIONSHIPS: *Overcoming Dinosaur Thinking*

Notes

CPSIA information can be obtained at www.ICGtesting.com
Printed in the USA
BVOW040511050412

286929BV00003B/1/P